"When God made Jerry Colonna, She threw away the mold. In his life and work—and in this book—Jerry is a remarkable combination of fierce and gentle, gravitas and humor, laserlike intellect and playful imagination. He knows that the unexamined life is not worth living. He also knows that if you choose to live such a life, you should never, ever take a job that involves other people. Jerry's way of working with leaders has nothing to do with 'seven steps to success' or posturing as an advocate for high-minded leadership virtues. Instead, he helps us untangle the inner knots with which we hobble first ourselves, then our colleagues, then the work we do, then the world. In these beautifully written pages—full of engaging stories, bedrock truths, and practical tools—you'll learn about Jerry's way of working, about the man himself, and about yourself. Life offers no guarantees, but I can come close to assuring you that this book will help heal you and transform the way you work to the benefit of all concerned. I'm one among many who can testify that that's just what Jerry does."

—Parker J. Palmer, author of *On the Brink of Everything*, *Let Your Life Speak*, and *The Courage to Teach*

"A few months into our nascent partnership, which we were calling Acme at the time but became Flatiron, Jerry and I got stuck in Boston due to bad weather. We decided to rent a car and drive home, figuring we could get home and sleep in our own beds. As with most late-night drives, the talk got real, and at one point, Jerry explained that as a young adult he had tried to take his life. My understanding of Jerry changed completely at that moment, and so did my appreciation for him. I've watched Jerry struggle, and ultimately come to terms, with his demons. And in the process, maybe because of it, he has become the most sought-after executive coach. This book tells the story of that and a lot more. Jerry's a role model for those who want to take the things that get in their way and turn them into the source of their strength. This book will help you do the same."

—Fred Wilson, co-founder and partner
of Union Square Ventures

"This book is filled with honesty, vulnerability, and insight, teaching us to be brave and to pursue radical self-inquiry to get to know ourselves, to be truthful with ourselves, and to love ourselves. In this pursuit, Jerry shines a light on a path that defines a healthier sense of what it means to be a leader. Countless books offer ways to become a better leader in the business world, but this is the only one with the insight and wisdom to offer a unique perspective: To be a better leader, you must be a better human."

—Bijan Sabet, co-founder and
general partner of Spark Capital

"*Reboot* flips everything on its head, showing that it takes grit and tenacity to be vulnerable. With insightful and emotional stories, Colonna shows how facing our pain head-on, with heart, can get us through to the other side. And how we can arrive there as more whole and hopeful beings. And, boy, can the world use that now. This book has inspired me to open up more, so that I can be more."

—Congressman Tim Ryan, U.S. House of Representatives, Ohio, and author of *Healing America*

"*Reboot* is filled with roller coasters, asteroids, and lemon drops; my copy is now dog-eared, underlined, filled with notes, and a bit banged up from all the times it was pulled in and out of my bag on flights. It is exactly what I had hoped it would be—the story of a brokenhearted warrior. It's Jerry's story, and it encouraged me to reflect on my own. Seat taken, he models the behavior of an elder I can see myself becoming. I thank him for being brave and openhearted enough to write it; he stuck his head in the mouth of the monster and showed all of us that we can do the same."

—Bryce Roberts, managing partner of OATV

"Jerry Colonna's *Reboot* takes us along on tough, inspiring journeys of self-discovery—his own, those of the people he's helped, and yours, if you're up to it. Startlingly candid stories from his business and personal life, along with insights from his study of the spiritual, complete his road map for aligning our values with our work."

—Anne Kreamer, author of *It's Always Personal* and *Risk/Reward*

"*Reboot* is a tour de force—brilliant, brave, and deeply emotionally resonant. It will inspire those who sorely need help—but don't seek it—to act. The description of the Loyal Soldier experience, for example, is quite compelling, beautifully capturing how we maintain painful and destructive parts of ourselves in order to survive. *Reboot* is powerful, penetrating, and psychologically masterful. It's a gift."

—Dr. Rory Rothman, Psya.D., LP

"This is a book about courage and love. Jerry bravely stands in front of his reader with a strong back and open heart. Rather than merely dispensing advice or sharing anecdotes, he models the kind leadership to which we can all aspire."

—Isaac Oates, CEO of Justworks

"*Reboot* is a book you can't put down, with lessons you'll want to revisit time and time again. By sharing his deeply personal experiences, Jerry uses his past as an instrument to help us find our own truths. He has given us the framework by which to carry forward uplifted and enlightened. I'm not only a better leader because of Jerry's honesty, I'm a better person—friend, mother, citizen."

—Sarah Kauss, founder and CEO of S'well

Reboot

Reboot

LEADERSHIP AND
THE ART OF GROWING UP

JERRY COLONNA

HARPER
BUSINESS

An Imprint of HarperCollins*Publishers*

HarperCollins books may be purchased for educational, business, or sales promotional use. For information, please email the Special Markets Department at SPsales@harpercollins.com.

FIRST EDITION

Title page illustration by Roobcio/Shutterstock, Inc.

Library of Congress Cataloging-in-Publication Data

Names: Colonna, Jerry, author.
Title: Reboot : leadership and the art of growing up / Jerry Colonna.
Description: New York : HarperBusiness, 2019.
Identifiers: LCCN 2018049676 | ISBN 9780062749536
Subjects: LCSH: Leadership. | Conscience, Examination of. | BISAC:
    BUSINESS & ECONOMICS / Leadership. | BUSINESS & ECONOMICS /
    Entrepreneurship. | BUSINESS & ECONOMICS / Workplace Culture.
Classification: LCC BF637.L4 C577 2019 | DDC 158/.4—dc23 LC record
    available at https://lccn.loc.gov/2018049676

19 20 21 22 23 LSC 10 9 8 7 6 5 4 3 2 1

To Sam, Emma, and Michael:
May you always feel loved, safe, and that you belong.
This is for you.

To Dr. Avivah Sayres:
You were right; I *did* have it in me.

CONTENTS

CONTENTS

FOREWORD

I first met Jerry at a dinner party hosted by a mutual friend, Jeff Walker. It was the kind of dinner party at which a single topic was put to the entire group for discussion. That night each of us was asked to describe a meaningful encounter with contemplative practice.

We listened quietly as the rotation went around the table. Jerry was up before me, and when he spoke, he referred to a very difficult period in his life, one in which a book called *Faith*, which I had written, was among the resources that had helped him. The word *faith*, as I had used it, did not mean belief or doctrine or dogma—I saw faith as being about connection—but our ability to connect to often hidden sources of strength within us, and our ability to connect to a picture of life bigger than just the immediate circumstances we see before us.

By the time Jerry finished speaking, he was crying, and I

was crying, too. It has always meant a lot to me when someone appreciates *Faith*. *Faith* had been a difficult book for me to write. It was the story of my own faith journey, and it demanded revelations of my deepest heart values, descriptions of my traumatic childhood, memories of my most significant moments of despair, and a vulnerability about things I somehow never found myself talking about ordinarily. My guide throughout that experience had been a quotation from the writer Dorothy Allison: "Write the story that you were always afraid to tell. I swear to you that there is magic in it, and if you show yourself naked for me, I'll be naked for you. It will be our covenant." Or, as a writer friend of mine urged me one stuck day, "Just tell the truth."

Jerry and I became good friends, and I was honored when he asked me to write this foreword. As soon as I began reading *Reboot: Leadership and the Art of Growing Up*, I saw his authenticity, compassion, and almost eerie acuteness of perception leap right off the page. I realized, "He really did tell the truth." That's what makes this book a generous and important offering.

Imbuing leadership with depth, resolve, congruency, and resilience—as Jerry describes in the following pages—inevitably involves discovering the adult within us: the capacity to face fears, to care about ourselves and others in a rare and potent balance, to be radically honest, to inquire within, and to listen to others. We discover that adult capacity, in all its poignancy and tenderness, and we bring it into the light of day, and we nurture it and help it to grow.

For most of us, that capacity is often hidden in the shadows, and not just hidden, but intricately entangled with our persistent yet often hidden feelings of unworthiness, our certainty of defeat, our fragmentation, our sense of isolation and emptiness, and our sense of overwhelm coupled with our conviction that we can never rest. Jerry's gift is in helping us navigate that landscape—to lean into that shadowy world and capture the treasures held there, all the while learning to be both strong and kind to ourselves and to others.

If the book you are writing is asking honesty and clear discernment of the reader, offering a path to a fulfilling and true and liberating life change, then you can't write from a supercilious perch or make yourself immune to self-revelation or imply that you have never struggled or had any difficulty perfectly manifesting the qualities you are talking about. You could try, of course, but it would show. What shows in contrast, in Jerry's book, is his own stripping away of armor or defensiveness or obfuscation. I could sense the validity in the comment one of Jerry's friends had made to him: "Writing this book is gonna kick your butt." I bet it did. Actually, I saw it did.

That's the beauty of determining if you are really going to speak from the heart: no imparting knowledge from on high, no separation from the many dilemmas and yearnings for success and even anguish of your audience. It's a powerful book, and a truly useful one, because Jerry kept that covenant. He got naked. He told the truth.

When Jerry first asked me to write the foreword, I was honored but uncertain. I asked, "Why not a mogul, a famous business success?" He replied that this wasn't an ordinary business book—it reconfigures notions of success itself and ideas of who we are and what would make us happy. It teaches us how, above all things, to be real. The journey laid out is a path to equanimity, or peace, which is priceless. The book is genuinely a transmission, heart to heart.

—*Sharon Salzberg*

DEDICATION OF THE MERIT

May all beings enjoy happiness and the root of happiness.

May we be free from suffering and the root of suffering.

May we not be separated from the great
happiness devoid of suffering.

May we dwell in the great equanimity free
from passion, aggression, and prejudice.

—A BUDDHIST PRAYER TO CULTIVATE THE FOUR IMMEASURABLES:
LOVINGKINDNESS, COMPASSION, EMPATHY, AND EQUANIMITY

Reboot

Introduction:
Elevating Darkness

I didn't set out to write a book about growing up. But, as those who've attempted to get their thoughts down on paper know, the true nature of the book revealed itself after I'd begun the excavations behind a simple question: What do I believe to be true about work, leadership, and how we may live our lives?

The simplicity of the answer startled me: I believe that better humans make better leaders. I further believe that the process of learning to lead well can help us become better humans. By growing to meet the demands of the call to leadership, we're presented with the chance to finally, fully, grow up.

Such revealed wisdom is often better than discovered wisdom. It's best, I suspect, because it comes from our lived experiences and the intrinsic and inherent depths of our being.

Moreover, such a revelation is better because it transforms us; it is a process that can come about only from learning to be still, learning to listen.

Standing still and powering down allow us to start anew and, if you will, reboot our core operating and belief systems. Standing still and listening deeply to our heart as well as to the hearts around us are the necessary first steps toward moving past merely, numbly, surviving our lives. As poet Terry Tempest Williams advises, we learn, then, to speak and "comprehend words of wounding without having these words become the landscape where [we] dwell." With such comprehending, we elevate the darkness of our lives, lead from the realm of the stars, and continue growing up.

I had a sense that this was true at the very first planning meeting for the book. Hollis Heimbouch, my editor (friend and teacher), and Jim Levine, my agent (friend and teacher), and I sat at a conference table in Jim's office to plot out the book. Earlier, Jim had shown me around his office, including a small room filled with Muppet-like puppets. Glancing quickly at the collection, one caught my attention. "Is that you?" I asked Jim. He laughed and said, somewhat shyly and with pride, "Yeah. That's me."

Back at the table, we sat together. My heart raced. I squirmed uncomfortably while sweating. We talked about the books on leadership that we admired. We spoke of writers who'd moved each of us. Jim spoke of the things I'd written, the questions I'd asked people to consider. "I love your simple, powerful questions, like 'What is work?'" he said. I was pleased but still nervous. My eyes darted between the two of them.

Hollis had a hand on a large stack of papers; my work, old blog posts, and an interview or two. "I love the way you provoke people. You get them to think differently."

As I looked from one to the other and back again, an insight struck me: "Wait. You don't want me to write a book of advice about the five things every entrepreneur should know about leadership?" Then—and this will surprise no one who really knows me—I burst into tears.

"Oh, no," said a surprised Hollis while looking to Jim. "Not at all. We want you to do *your* book." They wanted me to write the book I was supposed to write—*my* book.

My initial relief was quickly replaced by terror: I understood immediately that the excavations necessary to make sense of these intertwined and interdependent truths—that leadership requires an authentic and vulnerable dive into the wrecks of our lives—would force me to grow in ways I hadn't bargained for. After I started writing and began experiencing all sorts of uncomfortable memories and revelations, a dear friend warned, "Writing this book is gonna kick your butt." So it went and so it still goes.

The personal challenge didn't stem from coming to grips with writing well about the *how* of leadership. The challenge stemmed from the demand I'd placed on myself to show up fully, bravely, and to look inward without looking away. While it is true that to lead with depth, resolve, congruency, and resilience you must have the faith to look inward, it is equally true that to speak of such things without being willing to reveal your own actualization, your own journey to adulthood, would be hollow and empty. Hollow and empty would not suffice.

Turning the pursuit of purpose, mission, and leadership into the means to discover the adult lurking within us requires that we show up with radical authenticity. That "we" includes me. To live up to the belief that the pursuit of leadership requires a pursuit of growing up, we must be willing to work with that which arises in the pursuit. This includes that which arises whether we take our seat as a CEO, an author, or simply as ourselves, as we were born. I wouldn't ask you to do something that I am not willing to attempt myself.

Perhaps my touch hasn't been as light, deft, and skillful as I would have liked. Perhaps in my rush to share and grow, there's a weightiness to my words that I didn't consciously intend or wouldn't have chosen. Perhaps you'd prefer that I told you how to do the job rather than ask you why you'd like to do the job in the first place. Perhaps, then, I frustrate you. If so, forgive me. Sometimes, as my daughter Emma once observed, I ask the questions you'd rather not answer. Sometimes, though, my wish to elevate the darkness to the realm of the stars gets the better of me.

THE FORMULA

As often happens, I hit upon the insight I needed when I wasn't searching for it. A few years back I was pacing the room, thinking about the talk I was about to give. There were thirty people in stiff, uncomfortable chairs. As usual, my T-shirt was mildly sweaty. As usual, I was shoeless—discalced. I was struggling to explain coaching, struggling to explain why it was that, to help people lead well, I was pushing to help them know themselves better.

They were leaders, each of them. Some came from established organizations and were in the middle of their careers. Some were new to the demands of organizational leadership. All of them were struggling. All of them were there, in effect, for coaching.

With enthusiastic excitement and a touch of frustration, I grabbed some dry-erase markers and pulled a whiteboard to the front of the room. "It's like this . . . ," I shared as I began sketching in my indecipherable scrawl, "everyone is always looking for the 'how' to do things." And I wrote, "Practical Skills."

"But, really, they need to understand the 'why' of what they do, and ultimately, who they are," I continued, racing across the board, scrawling out, "Radical Self-inquiry."

"And when they do that, when they look in places they've avoided, they often get stuck," I continued. "They get scared. They get lost in their fears and in old patterns of self-loathing. So, mired in their self-criticism, they think they're the only one who hasn't a fucking clue as to what they are doing or how to live.

"Worse," I continued, "they're too damned afraid to admit that they're making shit up. And they stay stuck in these lonely leadership bubbles, spinning. Scared. Lonely. Afraid of being found out." My words hung in the air. I could feel their bodies tensing with fear. I knew they were holding their breath.

"But then someone is brave enough to go first. Some brave soul admits that she feels in trouble. And the tribe around her lets out their breath." The folks in the room, first-time CEOs, each of them, let out a collective breath. I wrote, "Sharing the experience with friends and peers" on the whiteboard and, as I wrote, I said, "and suddenly people realize they're not alone. And, even more, that if we're all feeling this way, then maybe, just maybe, the feelings may be true, but the facts may be inaccurate."

I turned back to the audience, pausing to let my words sink in: "You are not alone." A few folks begin to tear up. I turned to the board and sketched in plus signs between the statements, drew an equals sign underneath, as if I were creating a fraction, a mathematical formula. Under the line I wrote, "Enhanced leadership plus greater resiliency."

$$\frac{\text{Practical Skills Development + Radical Self-Inquiry + Shared Experiences}}{\text{Enhanced Leadership + Greater Resiliency}}$$

I then drew thick red lines under the word *resiliency*. "While I care about you being better leaders," I said, "I care more about you being able to survive. I want you to not make yourselves sick. I want you to be happy, to see your families, even to have families, to lay your head down on the pillow at night and rest in the belief that you are okay, that the world is okay, that all whom you love and care about are okay, and that even if things don't go as planned, you'll still be okay.

"I want you to not end up wondering if the world would be better off without you. I want you to have peace of mind." Resiliency, I stressed, is an antecedent to equanimity.

"Practical skills," I explained, "are the things that everyone believes necessary to succeed as leaders." They are the skills that describe the how of the job—the incredibly important, necessary, skills needed to grow and build organizations: How do you hire someone? How do you fire someone? How do you scale a team? How do you raise the capital to launch a business?

Discussing and encouraging people to share what they are going through often takes a little practice. I've got a well-earned reputation for making people cry and, in a sense, I helped found an executive coaching company, Reboot, to help folks do just that: to share what's really going on. Whether it's in individual sessions with a coach or at one of our "boot camps"—multi-day immersive experiences that folks have come to call "Reboots"—I and my colleagues explain that the secret to getting people to cry is simply to ask them to feel. Or, more specifically, ask them to slow down enough to notice how they are feeling. My radical, surprising, unprecedented question that always does the trick is quite simple; I ask, "How are you?" But then I follow it up with, "No. Really . . . how *are* you?" Not, I emphasize, the bullshit, throwaway line we toss at each other without thinking, the "I'm fine. How are you?" that passes for empathetic inquiry and honest conversation. I ask a genuinely curious, "How are you?" in a way that allows people to honestly inquire within and, equally important, share the response with others who have allowed themselves to be equally open.

"Start with a genuine 'How are you,'" I tell folks, "and then move on to describing the things—practical and existential—that are troubling you." Share with folks and, equally important, stay open and listen to their answers as well. Then simply notice how the isolation and overwhelm shift, even a tiny bit.

But the most challenging piece of the formula—indeed, the most important—is the notion of radically inquiring within. I define it as the process by which self-deception becomes so skillfully and *compassionately* exposed that no mask can hide us anymore. The notion is to recognize that, if things are not okay, if you're struggling, you stop pretending and allow yourself to get help. Even more, it's the process by which you work hard to know yourself—your strengths, your struggles, your true intentions, your true motivations, the characteristics of the character known as "you." The you behind the masks, the stories, the protective but no longer useful belief systems that have been presented for so long as the "you" that you would like everyone to see.

Invariably such inquiry involves getting to know, as the poet Adrienne Rich says, "not the story of the wreck but the wreck itself." With help, patience, courage, and guidance, we explore the wreck and retrieve the treasure. Knowing how to survive and understanding what it takes to thrive are skills that come from our childhood. Take any random group of entrepreneurs, for example, and do a quick unscientific survey by asking them to raise their hands if they grew up in an environment where at least one parent had disappeared or left or was never present. Most hands will shoot up. Early promotion into adulthood is often painful and equally often a sign of an early promotion into leadership. Probe a bit further and you may find that leaders who have built their company may have unconsciously stacked the team with other folks who experienced such early promotion.

Radically inquiring within allows us to step back and see the patterns of our lives not as random acts of a willful or even vengeful god but as forces that shape who we are. It's this understanding that will make us not only better leaders but better, happier, more resilient people.

NOT PRACTICAL BUT USEFUL

In writing this book, my goal is to provide an experience that allows you to do your work. I want you to experience being challenged to grow, to think about the structures of your life. Reading the book should feel like a coaching session or a boot camp, a time to step away from habitual and long-held patterns, using tools of inquiry that tap into your unconscious mind, unmask you, and that can enhance your sense of community, which is essential to healing. A well-asked question creates a sense of well-being even as it disrupts the story making that has protected us for so long.

As you read this book, I'd like you to hold these questions in your heart:

1. How did my relationship to money first get formed and how does it influence the way I work as an adult? What was the belief system around money and work that I grew up with? (Chapter 1.)

2. How can I lead with the dignity, courage, and grace that are my birthright? How can I use even the loss of

status and the challenge to my self-esteem that are inherent in leadership to grow into the adult I want to be in the world? (Chapter 2.)

3. In what ways have I depleted myself, run myself into the ground? Where am I running from and where to? Why have I allowed myself to be so exhausted? (Chapter 3.)

4. Who is the person I've been all my life? What can that person teach me about becoming the leader I want to be? What was the story my family told about being real, being vulnerable, being true? (Chapter 4.)

5. Why do I struggle so much with the folks in my life? Why are relationships so difficult? What am I not saying to my co-founder, my colleagues, my family members, my life partner that needs to be said? (Chapter 5.)

6. What's my purpose? Why does it feel I'm lost while I struggle to move forward? How do I grow, transform, and find meaning? (Chapter 6.)

7. How has who I am shaped the ways I lead others and myself? What are the unconscious patterns of my character structure that are showing up in my organizations? (Chapter 7.)

8. How might I survive my life of heartbreak? How might I live in peace? (Chapter 8.)

9. What kind of leader and adult am I? What is enough? How will I know when my job is done? (Chapter 9.)

As you read on, consider the lessons you have internalized about the risks and possibilities of being open, vulnerable, and real. What were you taught about being yourself? What has been the benefit of following that teaching? What was the cost?

Work gives us the means to create the physical safety upon which our lives depend. Work feeds and shelters us and those we love. Work can give us meaning. But work can also be a means of our suffering. By understanding what's truly happening all around us, the ways our core belief systems influence our everyday experience, we can extract meaning from the suffering, coax the lotus from the mud, as the Buddhists teach. But this will happen only if we use those challenges that the calls to leadership make on us, not only to grow up but also help us discover our why.

There are worthy, helpful, and pragmatic books that can help you focus on the how. In the end, I suppose, I've always found more helpful resources that have helped me unpack the whys of our lives. Helping people sort through the why of life helps them access all they need to know to answer the hows that work demands. The hows of life and leadership are endless. If you enhance your understanding of the why of who you are, you'll be able to face the unending uncertainty in the pursuit of the perfectly executed how. Moreover, if such inquiry is done well, with well-asked questions and deeply true answers, you will end up with a tailor-made how. Such work may not feel quite so practical at first, but it is undeniably useful.

This is the goal of this book. To be useful in understanding the why of your leadership. This is what I try to do with the leaders with whom I work every day. This is my wish for you.

THE SEEDBED FOR GROWTH

In the space between our memories and the stories we create about ourselves, we live our lives. We create our companies. We create our wishes and dreams and gather in those around us as our families and our communities.

Exploring that space between memories and the stories we create allows us to emerge as the leaders we were born to be. My journey as a leader has taught me that my childhood demanded a hypervigilance and that, to stay safe, I learned to work ceaselessly to try to make sense of the world (even as I was confronted with insensible acts and facts). As part of that effort, I listened closely—collecting and holding the stories of those around me as clues to a puzzling life.

The result is that I often see, hear, sense things that others miss. This can be a source of great wisdom. But this sensing can be an impediment to my peace of mind as well, for I can create whole ships of fiction out of the random flotsam and jetsam that float my way. Still, when I sit well and quietly, I can see a way through the puzzle, especially when another is blocked. I laugh as I recall that one of my favorite childhood pastimes was completing books of mazes. I like working my way out of mazes; I am good at it.

Among the many things I have seen and experienced is the wisdom of elders, those who have come before me; elders such as my longtime psychoanalyst Dr. Avivah Sayres, my Buddhist teacher Sharon Salzberg, and my dear friend and soul brother, Parker Palmer. Watching my elders age, I have come to understand the wisdom of not only growing up but aging gracefully, and for one, entering death—the thing I fear most of all—with courage and humor.

I suspect such elder-wisdom stems from inquiring into the nature of suffering and your formation. It manifests in a more complete understanding of your life, and when your work is done. "Enough," as Parker, writes in a beautiful poem called "Harrowing," "The Job is done."

Such elder-wisdom seeps into and strengthens my bones. There's a wisdom in being able to discern when the job is done. For the job to be done, we must know that it's time to let go of the striving to become and allow ourselves the restful grace of simply being. In my effort to simply be, I've learned to balance the disquietude of the past with the life-giving excitement of the future, the seedbed for the growing to come.

Harrowing

by Parker J. Palmer

The plow has savaged this sweet field
Misshapen clods of earth kicked up
Rocks and twisted roots exposed to view
Last year's growth demolished by the blade

I have plowed my life this way
Turned over a whole history
Looking for the roots of what went wrong
Until my face is ravaged, furrowed, scarred.

Enough. The job is done.
Whatever's been uprooted, let it be
Seedbed for the growing that's to come.
I plowed to unearth last year's reasons—
The farmer plows to plant a greening season.

CHAPTER 1

Passing GO

Mom was my Monopoly buddy.

When I was a boy, Mom and I spent hours playing Monopoly. To this day, I love rainy days, in part, because back then, when it rained, we'd spend the day playing board games, from Chutes and Ladders to The Game of Life. But I loved Monopoly most of all.

I loved that it could take hours to play properly (not the "shortened" version, where you dealt out the cards representing properties, but the *right* way . . . the way according to the rules . . . where you collected properties only after landing on them and buying or trading them). I loved collecting those deeds. I loved being the thimble, the iron, the dog.

I loved passing "Go" and collecting $200. I felt great about amassing money but, most of all, I loved surprising people with what I was capable of doing.

When I was a boy, I wasn't often seen. I was looked after, cared for. I was held and comforted, especially after some painful experience. But I wasn't often *seen*. I was a good boy when inside I wanted to rage. I tried hard, all the time, when inside I wanted not to care. I was compliant, and therefore complicit, in not being fully appreciated.

When I was a boy, and we played Monopoly, everyone would lay out money in front. Piles of currency neatly stacked and sorted: $500s, $100s, $50s, and so on. Not me, though. I'd keep all my money stacked together, under the game board. I didn't need to lay it out in front of me to know my worth. I'd keep track in my head of how much I had. And I'd surprise everyone by buying up their properties when they were bankrupt. I'd surprise them with my cleverness and cunning.

When my cunning, my skills, my ability to understand and work with money would be revealed, I'd feel seen not for being good—quiet, compliant, a "good boy"—but for being me—a good person who was also smart and skillful.

What's more, at seven, I came to understand that, while people might not *see* you, might not *get* you, you could use that fact to survive.

The Game of Life, Hi! Ho! Cherry-O, and Monopoly taught me about life.

I learned, for example, that you needed money to win, to be safe, to never be hungry. With it, you could buy real estate, you could put little green houses on those properties, and then, over time, generate more money. If you played the game right, you could generate enough to make sure that Mom and Dad didn't fight about having enough food. Dad wouldn't yell at Mom if you took more than two Oreos.

There were nine of us in the two-bedroom apartment on the ground floor of a small Brooklyn building owned by my grandfather. I was born in December 1963, a month after JFK was killed. By then, my oldest siblings, Vito and Mary, were already beginning to cycle in and out of the house. While the same small space was home for all of us, it was rare that we'd all be there at the same time.

Dad was a foreman at a printing company, a place at which he had worked since high school (and to which he came back after serving in the army). Mom stayed home with us.

Dad was a good man whose broken heart sometimes led him to drink to drunkenness. Mom was a good woman whose broken childhood led to mental illness that further led her to hear and see things that, as often as not, weren't there.

Together, they had more kids than they could afford, financially as well as emotionally. Being number six of seven, I grew up wondering whether it was I who had tipped the scales, broken the camel's back. I worried I was the mouth that was one too many to feed; the one who caused the whole lot of us to never have enough to feel safe, warm, and happy.

My mother's father, Dominic Guido, was an iceman. He sold ice in the summer, coal in the winter, and homemade wine all year long. Mom always said his shoulders were covered with hair to protect his body from the fifty-pound blocks of ice he carried up the stoops of houses in Brooklyn. He'd dropped out of school in the sixth grade, in his home village in Italy, Palo del Colle, just outside Bari. He'd made his way to the States and become an entrepreneur—someone no venture capitalist would ever fund, even though he understood the most important principle of business: end the day with more money than you began it.

Grandpa always seemed to have enough and even a little extra to spare for us. He owned the building where my family lived, the same building where my mother and then later my sisters would mop the hallways. Grandpa would visit on Saturdays, usually bringing food. My father would stiffen as Grandpa came down the hallway and into our apartment, filling the room with the smell of woolen underwear and Old Spice.

Grandpa and Dad had a hard relationship. There were a few possible reasons.

From Grandpa's perspective, I could see how he might have blamed Dad for their having had all of us. Mom was pregnant with my brother Vito, after all, when they got married. "She had too many kids," I imagine him thinking, "that's why she was sick." And, of course, to their Catholic eyes, it was a sin that Mom was pregnant before marriage: "She sinned, that's why she got sick." Devoutly religious, Mom must have been racked by guilt. I can hear her assuaging her guilt now: "I would have had a dozen," she'd say all the time, speaking of us kids, "if only the doctors would have let me."

Maybe, from Grandpa's point of view, it was Dad's beers. She would yell all the time about his drinking (which worsened after his time in the army), right after they were married.

In manic moments, Mom would slam the table and focus on Dad's two six-packs of Pabst Blue Ribbon a night. When she was kind, she'd guess that the stench of the Nazi death camps he'd visited in postwar Germany caused him to drink. When she was unkind, she poked at the fact that he wasn't really Italian, that he'd been adopted by an Italian family and he was really a drunk German or Irishman.

"If only he weren't a drunk," I can hear Grandpa saying to himself, "then my daughter wouldn't be sick."

But maybe the tension between Grandpa and Dad was rooted in the family splits that went all the way back to the pale limestone of Palo del Colle outside of Bari. In that tiny village, both Dad's mother, Mary Colonna, and Mom's mother, Nicoletta Guido, were cousins. But not just cousins; they were rivals. As a girl, Mary was orphaned and raised by her aunt. Nicoletta and Mary were, in a sense, sisters.

To heighten the tensions, each of them married an iceman; Mary married Vito who was never the entrepreneur that Dominic was.

If I were forced to guess, I think Grandpa blamed Dad for Mom's illness. Her delusions, her mania, her depression started around the time they got married. "If only she'd married someone else, had had a different life, was able to go to art school as she'd hoped," I imagine him saying, "then maybe my baby girl wouldn't be sick." As a father now, my heart aches when I think of him worrying about his baby girl, my mother.

I weep when I think of Grandpa, helpless and angry, watching his baby, his seventh of seven children, being strapped into a straitjacket and carted away to a hospital to have her memories and suffering mind jolted with electroshock therapy again and again. And again.

It's hard, even, to imagine his feelings as his daughter's seven children were divvied up among her siblings and how he and my grandmother would take in my brother John and me.

Even when Mom wasn't in the hospital, John and I would visit Grandpa and Grandma on Wednesdays after school. Their house smelled wonderful: of lemon drops kept in a tin in the hallway cupboard with the pale green door; of coffee ground with a hand-cranked grinder that hung on a kitchen wall beneath a photo of the saint, Padre Pio; and, in summer, of newly cut roses from Grandma's garden and figs picked from the tree growing next to the porch at the back of their kitchen—a tree brought as a sapling from Palo del Colle and protected from winter by being wrapped in blankets and old rugs, with a bucket on top to keep the rain and snow out.

Such smells still drop me to my knees. I pass a tree whose springtime blossoms are just bursting out and am teleported, instantly, to Brooklyn's Prospect Park on a cool April morning. The oddly tangy metallic smell of Coppertone sunscreen still makes me feel as if I've got grains of beach sand stuck in my teeth . . . remnants of the bologna sandwiches Mom would make for our trips to Coney Island. Smells bypass the cognitive, adult parts of my brain and go directly to my soul.

The smells of coffee, roses, and lemon drops signal I'm safe.

I grind whole beans and once again I'm five years old, snuggled into Grandma's lap, my head on her bosom, rocking in her arms, safe, warm, and happy. Grandma and Grandpa's house was my sanctuary from the chaos of home.

To my child's heart, money meant roses, fresh figs, ground coffee, and lemon drops, forever. Money was safety. The pursuit of money, then, became a chase for safety and a flight from poverty, chaos, and the streets of my childhood.

"What will it take?" Dr. Sayres, my psychoanalyst asks me nearly forty years later. "When will you stop?"

I was in my thirties—a father, a success—and I would lie on her couch, staring at the ceiling. I'd been staring at that damn ceiling for seven or eight years already.

"Bill Gates," I sputter, shocked at my own response. I never thought of myself as pursuing Gates-like wealth. I liked to think I was above that.

But as I lay there, I had to admit that, to the little boy who'd spent Sunday dinners hiding out under the dining room table, becoming Bill Gates–rich would mean lemon drops forever.

Money, of course, brought with it admiration. People thought I was smart because I had money. Some of these same folks had dismissed me when it seemed that all I'd amount to would be poet or college professor—wise but poor. Money, success in business, had given me access to power. Suddenly, it seemed, my opinion mattered to businesspeople, to politicians, to leaders of all sorts. To the people who, as a boy, I barely knew existed when I played scully, shooting bottlecaps filled with crayon wax on boards carved into the asphalt of East 26th Street in Flatbush, Brooklyn.

Money and success meant admiration, acknowledgment, accolades. Money and success came to seem ends unto themselves.

I wasn't completely delusional, of course. And I wasn't entirely enraptured by money. There was always enough of the poet inside me to remind me of the falsity of those goals.

As with Monopoly, the pursuit of success in business became a game, something to pursue for gratification of the intellect. "See," I'd quietly whisper to myself, "I'm not just a schmuck from Flatbush. I can run with the big dogs."

Success and money—and even more important, the *busyness* needed to create those—became proof of my worth as a human.

BILL GATES, LEMON DROPS, AND ME

It surprised me that becoming rich would lead me to want to kill myself.

But there I was, standing on the lip of the smoking, stinking hole of Ground Zero. After the 9/11 attack, I had agreed to two things: the first, to join JPMorgan as a venture capital investor; and the second, to serve as a co-executive director for New York City's Olympic Bid committee.

The former was a plot to scoop up lemon drops. The latter was intended to somehow help New York, my home, my city, recover and for me to be seen as the hero I yearned to be.

In the weeks following the attacks, I'd lain awake at night, anxious. I managed the anxiety by trawling through survival websites, looking for emergency ration kits and creating "go" bags of food, water, medical supplies—everything my family and I would need if New York were to be attacked again.

In this hurting state of mind, I began working at JPMorgan and dived deep into raising money for the Olympic bid effort. I was good at both jobs. Moving to JPMorgan from my former venture capital firm, Flatiron Partners, where I had already amassed a track record as a smart investor (and managed to be beloved at the same time), I immediately made some good deals that within a year or two returned three to five times the capital we'd invested.

The fund-raising went well. I made appearances throughout the city drumming up support for the Olympic bid. I remember showing up at a community center in Flushing, Queens, raising money from a local chapter of the IBEW (the International Brotherhood of Electrical Workers). "They didn't just attack our country," I'd say, imitating a preacher as I walked the room, "they attacked our home. A city where one hundred eighteen languages are spoken among our 1.2 million schoolkids. They attacked your family. They attacked my family. They attacked us."

But on this day, I teetered on the edge of Ground Zero, among the piles that were, just months before, the twin towers of the World Trade Center. The ping, ping, ping of heavy equipment whose gears had been thrown in reverse rang out; bulldozers moved piles of shattered glass, shrapnel, and the smashed remains of people who, months before, were just trying to make enough money to buy their kids lemon drops.

Wall Streeters pass a frozen me as though I were just another of the thousands of ghosts haunting the streets of lower Manhattan. Panic fills my lungs, choking out the air. I wear a suit and tie to signify my power. I am rich. I have a beautiful family. I'm well respected. I even have a new sense of purpose—"Look at me. Look at how helpful to my City, I am. I am a good boy." I have all the lemon drops I could ever want. And, still, the old seen-but-not-seen feelings remain. I still can't shake the sense that I am hollow, not really occupying the meat bag that is me. I'm in my life but not really living. So why bother? I ask myself. I want to die.

My head swirls. I want to run downstairs to the subway platform and hide. Instead, I reach for my cell phone and call Dr. Sayres in Great Neck.

"Get in a cab and come see me," she says, taking control. "Get here now."

Over the coming weeks, we'd talk about what was happening to me. Being there but not really being there. Living a life of there-but-not-there hurt like hell.

And we'd talk about money, success, Bill Gates, and lemon drops.

The attacks on 9/11 hurt me. Like so many people, I was scared. The night before the attacks, I'd gone to Yankee Stadium to see my Yanks take on the damn Red Sox. Roger Clemens was going for his twentieth win that season and I had great seats. The game was rained out.

Nevertheless, I stayed in Manhattan that night, away from my home on Long Island. The next morning, September 11, I had an early-morning flight to Washington. I was having breakfast with some senators when the news of the attacks came in.

As with many, that day remains with me. A blurry haze of

feelings and memories . . . desperation to get home to my family in New York. Desperate to find out if those I loved were safe, warm, and happy.

But that's not what really drove me to the edge that day in 2002, a few months after the attack. It was the hollowness of my life itself. It was the realization that, despite having more lemon drops than I could have imagined, my heart still hurt.

It would take many more years to talk through all that had formed me, to sort through the bags I'd been carrying since childhood. These were my particular habits of mind; the experiences, patterns, and beliefs, that had led me to seek safety and solace through a real-life game of Monopoly by amassing as much money as I could, by grabbing lemon drops, and by constantly comparing my success to that of Bill Gates. This was *my mess*, my messy baggage, and now, at forty, I was going to have to start taking inventory. I was going to have to start sorting it out. There was no place to hide.

When I was in high school I studied photography and filmmaking. I remain fascinated by the fact that film is deceptive. What appears to be fluid, ongoing, and always in motion is, in fact, a series of still moments viewed incredibly quickly. Just like life itself.

What appears fluid is twenty-four frames per second. Twenty-four precious moments per second, lived second after second after second. And each of those still moments is imbued with feelings and memories. The rapid fluidity of each of those moments defines the patterns and beliefs that, in turn, define our lives.

Our lives are twenty-four frames per second, with each

frame a set piece of feeling, belief, obsession about the past, and anxiety about the future. Neither good nor bad, these frames form us. They become the stories we tell ourselves again and again to make sense of who we're becoming, who we've been, and who we want to be.

Ghosts of our pasts—our grandparents and their grandparents as well as the ghosts of their lives—inhabit the frames. They and their beliefs, interpretations of scenes, words, and feelings haunt the frames of lives as surely as the roses, figs, and lemon drops of our present daily lives do.

Slowing down the movie of our lives, seeing the frames and how they are constructed, reveals a different way to live, a way to break old patterns, to see experiences anew through radical self-inquiry.

POLE-CLIMBING MONKEYS

Late into a first conversation with a coaching client, I listen deeply for ghosts in the frames of his life.

"Jerry, I'm sixty-four and I need to figure out what I'll be doing with my life after I retire." He's wealthy enough. He's certainly successful enough. And he's an incredibly well-regarded public figure.

"Tell me about your decision to take that job in Baltimore fifteen years ago," I ask, following my intuition.

"It's funny that you ask about that," says my client, a little shocked. "My father told me it was the worst decision of my life . . . that I was going to regret that decision forever. He said, 'If you do this, you'll be raising the white flag on your career.'"

Suddenly I'm thrust back to being twenty-two. I've been working at the magazine for two years, since my college-age summer internship began. I'm being recruited to be a speech-writer and an aide to the CEO of NCR, in Dayton, Ohio. I turn to my Dad for advice: "Remember, Jerry, the higher up the pole the monkey climbs, the more his ass shows."

His fear, my father's fear, is clear. Stay low. Stay outta sight. Stay safe.

"I don't know what you should do when you retire," I say, returning to my client. "But I'll be happy to be your thought partner as you work it through.

"That said," I continue, "I suspect that it's time to no longer make decisions based on your father's fear. To no longer avoid his disapproval or to seek his approval. That feels like a good place to start this inquiry."

Or we can keep trying to put them aside, to ignore them, to shove the baggage of our lives into storage, unsorted, heavy, taking up more room with each year.

Tracing forward from these remembrances of things past gives us the chance to re-experience and reframe these beliefs. Doing so liberates us from the confounding forces we label as fate, destiny, or—even more frequently—the other person's "fault." We will never sort through them all, of course, but what we don't sort through impedes our happiness. It tricks us into using the rest of our lives—and the people we love, the professions we choose, the organizations we lead—to try to close the gaping wounds from childhood.

THE SAFETY OF TREES

On a hot summer morning, I stand in the shade of the dying horse chestnut tree, its five-fingered leaves, each with a saw-tooth edge, shade and cool the air. I am seven.

When it rains hard, the fattest nuts fall from the branches, their spikes, thick, hard, and sharp; their green skin veined with brown spots and worms.

The warm rain slips from leaf to leaf as I sit beneath the hundred-foot-tall tree. In its trunk is a crack, just big enough for me to hide in. I love the rain. I love being in, but not quite all the way in, the rain. The tree is my favorite hiding spot.

The tree's flowers are white and pink, and the leaf clusters that look so much like hands have unfolded as if in prayer. Wet/not wet. Warm/not warm. In but out. Seen but not seen. Safe but scared.

Inside the building, behind the bay windows of our ground-floor apartment, Mom and Dad are arguing again. She's accusing him, again, of having an affair. Again, he sits there silently. Again, I wait for it, his explosive response. She speaks so loudly that our entire inner life spills out onto East 26th Street. The bay windows can't contain their pain.

Pablo, who smeared dog shit on my face just the week before, walks by and jeers at me. Even today, I see his leering face, with his gash of a mouth and tongue stuck out. Five years older than me, and maybe a foot taller, Pablo always scared me.

He seemed to love to torture us younger kids. He loved to taunt me, to get me so angry that my face would swell and redden, and I'd stand in the middle of the asphalt screaming in fury.

One day he stuck a branch from the chestnut tree into a steaming pile of shit and chased me around and around a red car, my head spinning in fear, the air scraping my throat as I desperately tried to outrun Pablo and the stick. Such were the games little boys played on East 26th Street.

Over time the crack in the tree's trunk would grow, and the city would cut it down. Half-dead, it had become misshapen and distorted, unsafe to passersby. But right then, as a child, I wanted nothing more than to disappear into that crack, to escape the sounds coming from our house, to escape the taunts and humiliations of childhood, to shove it all aside.

The boy under the tree, hiding to feel safe, wishing for lemon drops, wishing to be found. Found but not found out. Because if I were found out, *they* might not like what they saw.

For being myself was never good enough. Being myself wouldn't stop Mom and Dad from fighting. It wouldn't guarantee we would have enough money. It wouldn't stop Dad from going out to John's Grocery Store for two six-packs of Pabst Blue Ribbon every night. It wouldn't stop Mom from talking to Jesus or to the late Bobby Kennedy. And it failed to keep her from saying she was going to kill herself, again and again and again.

And if being myself wasn't good enough to keep me lemondrop safe, how could I ever have been comfortable in my skin as a leader? How could I take my seat as an adult? How could I grow up?

CHOOSING TO BECOME ME

Money. Safety. Shame. A sense of belonging. A desire for escape. The fear of being found out. The fear of not being seen, of not being known and accepted for who I am. A desire to please. These paradoxes, these secrets, continue to shape us. But who we choose to be is awakened by the truths we choose to tell.

There are no epiphanies, no immediate radical discoveries that will suddenly and without work unwind the twisted balls of yarn that define our lives. But there are knowable moments, and seeing those knowable moments, and the ghosts they give rise to, can help us—children no more—become the adults we want to be. This is radical self-inquiry. This is the practice of making something good out of the accumulation of losses and false narratives that we all experience.

"I am not what has happened to me," taught Carl Jung. "I am what I choose to become."

But choosing requires knowing. It requires knowing how what happened to us influences the choices we made and continue to make. Again and again I ask my clients, "How are you complicit in creating the conditions of your lives that you say you don't want?"

But even more, in what ways does that complicity *serve* you? How does it serve my soon-to-be retired client to remain disconnected from himself such that he doesn't know how he'd like to spend his days? In what ways does it serve him to continue the battle for his father's approval and against his father's disapproval?

We've gathered, as we often do, on the first night of one of my company's boot camps. We gather folks to help them learn to lead by coming to know themselves better. The knowing-themselves-better can be so painful that we liken the process to boot camp, a rigorous training ground.

We sit safely in a circle. I read a poem. Tears are flowing in the small circle as they come to what will be the first of many recognitions: They are not alone. They are not alone in their fear, in their shame, in feeling unmoored and lost. We are here for radical self-inquiry, I tell them, because that is the path of authenticity and that path leads to resiliency.

"What the fuck are we doing listening to a poem," one camper yells, his faced twisting in anger. "I didn't come here to listen to goddamn poetry. I came here to be a better CEO. I have a greedy son-of-a-bitch head of sales and he's driving everyone crazy and I don't know what to do about him. That's why I'm here."

I've seen this resistance before; I stay steady. "I'll make a deal with you," I say, "If you stay through the weekend and if, at the end of the weekend, you don't know what to do with him, I'll give you your money back."

He calms down. Two days later we're deep into it. I've asked everyone to look at their own lives, to look at the companies they've created, the conditions they say they don't want. I turn to the camper with the greedy head of sales. I shock him, "Tell me about the shame."

He looks up, his eyes marked by the pain of a hard, hard life.

"I was a teenager when I ran away," he says, tears streaming.

"I started drinking then. I ended up living under an overpass."

"Tell me about the night and the promise you made to yourself," I prompt.

He's startled. His eyes ask, "How did you know?"

He says out loud, "It was raining, and I was cold . . ."

He goes on to explain that he'd sworn that he was never going to be cold or hungry or alone again. I nod in recognition. I see him as he sees himself more fully.

"Who hired the sales guy?"

He looks around sheepishly. "I did."

"And who promoted him?"

"Me," says the camper.

"There is nothing to be ashamed of," I tell him. "The problem isn't his greed. He's just doing what you hired him to do. You outsourced your need to never be cold and hungry again to someone more acceptable. And he's doing a great job at that."

"What if you took back your greed," I ask him, "and instead see it for what it truly is: a desire to be safe, warm, and happy?"

Take back the wish, take back the promise you made to yourself, leave aside the shame and own the fear not as something to deny but as something that fuels you.

He brightens. I continue: "Let's expand that view now. Let's go beyond making sure that you and your family are never hungry again. Let's see the ways you and your company have made it possible for your employees and their families to not be hungry. To feel safe, warm, and happy."

His body unfolds, and we all bear witness to his taking his seat not merely as a CEO but as a man, capable of providing for the boy under the overpass.

Radical self-inquiry is how we learn to become *more of* ourselves, *more like* ourselves, more authentic. More human.

And better humans are better leaders.

This is what great leaders do. Great leaders look unflinchingly in the mirror and transform untamed hungers and unruly compulsions into moments of self-compassion and understanding. In doing so, they create the spaces for each of us to do the same, turning our organizations into places of growth and self-actualization. They infuse the profanity of work with the sacred duty of Work: the opportunities to lead, to grow into their whole selves while nurturing others, encouraging them to do the same.

It would be easy to paint my realization around work as sacred duty as something sprung from some genius within. It was not. It sprang from exhaustion, from being lost myself, from having nowhere else to turn with my own suffering.

There's a story of the Buddha coming to realize the Four Noble Truths—the four foundational beliefs of Buddhism. In the story, he comes to these profound realizations after years of wondering and wandering, seeking answers. In my mind, though, the Buddha is from Flatbush, Brooklyn. When he finally comes to this moment, it's with utter desperation and more than a little anger.

"Fuck it," I hear him say to himself, "I can't figure out shit. And I'm just gonna sit under this bodhi tree until either I die or it makes sense." And so, he sits.

So, I sat. I'd walked away from a job, a title, status, and the pursuit of passing Go and collecting my next $200. I sat until I began to glimpse the ways I had been complicit in creating the conditions I said I didn't want. I sat until I began to realize that acknowledging these things within myself was the first step to really being seen—to having the thing I'd wished for all my life.

My noble truth, I'm humbled to admit, didn't come from within me. It came from the simple act of choosing to continue to live. Between the thing that triggers us and our unconsciously chosen action is a tiny bit of space. We grow in such spaces. We radically inquire within in those spaces. Sitting still, we get to see the spaces between the frames of lives speeding by and, as a result, see the whole movie with an unattached eye.

In sitting under my bodhi tree, I quietly came to find my truest calling.

My friend, the poet Pádraig Ó Tuama, says, "To live well is to see wisely and to see wisely is to tell stories." I'll go further; telling stories helps us live well. Telling the stories of our lives, telling the stories of the lives around us, helps us make sense of the world and, in the end, be wise.

Wise and sacred. Years ago, as I was beginning to distance myself more fully from that day, in 2002, when I teetered on the edge of my own Ground Zero, I was alone, naked, in a desert in southern Utah. On the second day of a three-night water-only fast, as part of a fourteen-day quest, I settled into the meaning of the true name I'd be given: Holder. Holder of Stories of the Heart. Holder of my stories. Holder of the stories of those I love. Holder of the stories of the brokenhearted leaders who come to me.

On that second day, I woke with terrible pains in my stomach. I'd had plenty of water, but the lack of food was breaking me down. The day before, I'd stripped down to as few clothes as I could bear. It was a relief to have as little as possible between me, the true me, and the Earth itself. But the bare skin left me raw. The lack of food left me weak, tired, and emotionally spent. I looked up to a cluster of boulders and saw a face. Grandfather Boulder, I named him. I asked him about my life.

"Holder," he taught me, "listening opens that which pain has closed.

"You were not given this life only to lament," he went on. "Make holy that which you were given: Go and listen."

Listening, I've come to understand, is bearing witness to lives unfolding, to lives being discovered. Deep listening, listening compassionately, means guiding, gently nudging, or sometimes shoving people down the path of radical self-inquiry so they can make their way to their own truest selves. Then, and only then, can they lead with the dignity and grace of being human.

The goal, then, is to help you listen to the stories of *your* heart so that, in the end, you can know the why of your leadership journey and become the adult, the full human you were meant to be. Then the simple but hard task becomes clear: Lead from the place of your truest self. Do so not merely for yourself but for those who love and entrust their careers to you.

The process of radical self-inquiry into one's own leadership journey is supported by standing still and taking the time to ask oneself open, honest questions around the rules we carry. Following each chapter will be a series of questions to prompt your own inquiry. Consider these as invitations to inquire within.

Journaling Invitations

How did my relationship to money first get formed?

———————

How did that relationship shape the work I've chosen
and my definitions of success and failure?

———————

How does it shape my view of the quality
of others' work and contributions?

———————

What was the belief system around money
and work that I grew up with?

———————

How does that impact my view of my own worthiness?

———————

CHAPTER 2

The Crucible and the Warrior

Of course, the night would be perfect; the stars crisp and achingly bright, the lulling cadence of cars crossing into Brooklyn from Manhattan over Colonel Roebling's wondrous bridge, the ka-thump, ka-thump, ka-thump of tires hitting expansion joints.

Even here on the roof deck of an old Jehovah's Witnesses building, some eight floors above the streets of Dumbo, the air is tinged with a faint mix of lilac, honeysuckle, and diesel exhaust. I'm sitting on a picnic table while Chad Dickerson sips from a bottle of beer. Of course, of course, of course . . . the night would be sweet *and* bitter. Tomorrow Chad will announce to the world that he's been asked to step down as CEO of Etsy, the online marketplace for handcrafted goods he had led for the past six years.

I am here to listen, to bear witness to and hold the story of this bittersweet moment. It's painful to watch my client, my friend, confront this new reality. Although he'd done many things right, although he'd grown into a leader with heart and authenticity, he was being fired.

His pain hangs in the air. And because my vocation is to be with people in their joy and their suffering, to hold myself as a container for them to work through such moments, my pain is exquisite—beautiful, delicate, sharp, piercing my heart like a needle. Nevertheless, there's no place I'd rather be than here, with him, with this pain. "Listening," I remember, "opens that which pain has closed."

I watch his eyes—I always watch my clients' eyes. Our eyes moist with memories, we talk of the time six years before. Just a few weeks into the job, he'd called me on his walk home from the office. The sudden reality of being CEO had churned the bile of his self-doubt and he'd vomited.

"Oh, Jerry," he said then. "Help me. I can't do this."

"Yes, you can," I'd told him then.

"Oh, Jerry," he says to me now, turning his weary, beaten-down eyes to me, "I did a good job, didn't I?"

"Yeah. Yeah, you did," I assure him.

We met regularly for most of those six years. Usually in his office, surrounded by handmade Etsy things—a cutting board in the shape of New York State, hand-polished cherry guitar picks, and coasters made to look like handmade cherry guitar picks. Outside the office, monstrous AC ducts had been wrapped in knitted covers to mask the ugly metal.

Sometimes we met in a conference room even more beautifully decorated. I won't forget the quilted and stuffed faux deer head mounted on the wall, as if after a kill. We'd talk of practical challenges. The difficulty of building an executive team when the company had such a profound history of dysfunction and a culture where all things that smacked of traditional business were (rightfully) suspect.

How do you attract a CFO, a general counsel, or a head of marketing when the culture finds such functions an anathema? How do you hold the heart of what is special, embracing the rebels and misfits who define the greatness of your organization, while creating a tolerant and caring space for those who've built their career on doing well at more traditional companies?

Back on the roof, I'm startled. I see something familiar but new in Chad, something powerful, something even more important than success or failure as a CEO. Years before, I'd given him the metaphor I often use with clients: "Take your seat." "Sit like royalty in your leadership seat," I say. "Sit as if you've the right to be there."

Over time, he'd done just that. He'd taken his seat, the company had grown, he'd built a powerful team, and the stomach churning had subsided. He did this by looking at his own *stuff*, through radical self-inquiry.

WELCOME TO THE NOT-KNOWING

Clients come to me seeking the answers. "How the hell do I do this job?" they ask either implicitly or explicitly. They act as if there's a playbook, a secret handbook that will teach them everything they need to know about leading.

The worst are the high achievers, the folks who made it through school by quickly figuring out what it took to get an A and then delivering whatever the teacher wanted. Figure out the rules, they'd learned, and succeed. And when they're given the task of leading and they can't figure out the rules, the vomit-inducing panic takes over.

This situation is nailed by a wonderful scene near the end of the seven-year run of the TV show *Mad Men*. Peggy, who's finally fully in charge, turns to her old boss, Don, for help. Don, who's about to leave the world of mad men forever, has emerged as a brokenhearted sage.

Don: I want you to feel good about what you're doing, but you'll never know. That's just the job.
Peggy: What's the job?
Don: Living in the "not-knowing."

Clients come to me because the "not-knowing" is so unbearable. I often make them crazy when I tell them the answer isn't in a book. "There's no book," I say, often nearly preaching. "There's no 'way,' no 'path,' that's been kept hidden from you." Some of them get angry when I ask them about their past or what's in their heart.

But I know that the truest path, the only way, for a warrior to emerge is through the path of radical self-inquiry, the process by which the mask is compassionately stripped away until there's no place left to hide.

On the roof, again, watching Chad, reassuring him, I realize he's gone beyond taking his seat as a CEO. He's grown into something calmer, steadier. He'd become not merely the man he'd always intended to be, the man he chose to be, but a gentle, brokenhearted warrior who leaned into his own pain to find the strength to do what is right.

Both of us had learned of his termination only a few days before. I thought about how he carried himself over those last few days, about how—despite having been fired—he'd worked late into the night to get the data right, to care for his colleagues, to tend to the company as he'd always done.

"What would Obama do?" we took to asking each other in moments when his heart flagged. How do you handle yourself on the way out, regardless of whether you were given the respect you deserved?

The back of the warrior is strengthened by knowledge of knowing the right thing to do. The soft, open heart is made resilient by remembering who you are, what you have come through, and how those things combine to make you unique as a leader.

"What would Obama do?" became both a rallying cry and an inside joke. What standards of dignity do you hold yourself to, regardless of how things unfold? What do the people who have counted on you to lead them need from you at this moment?

These questions shaped our inquiry into how he should handle what had transpired. His desire for radical self-inquiry had enabled him to ask (and to answer), "What kind of leader am I?"

Indeed, the simple act of asking, "What kind of leader am I?" implicitly acknowledges that there is no one way to lead.

I thought of the all-nighters he and his team had pulled, missing their families as they faced tasks at hand—cutting budgets, finding the savings. Again, I thought of Carl Jung: "I am not what has happened to me. I am what I choose to become." Looking ahead to how Chad would carry himself as the news became public—as he passed the baton to his successor; as he fielded questions from his team, his colleagues, his coworkers, his friends, and his family—I knew he'd sit regally, steady even in his shaky vulnerability.

I knew he would be transparent about his pain, but I didn't realize that the dignity with which he communicated would make him the epitome of grace.

Turning to his face, this weary soul with a beer in his hand, his gray hair in need of a trim, I could see it more clearly. "Oh, shit," I muttered to no one in particular, "this is his crucible moment." This was Chad's rite of passage, as leadership expert Warren Bennis put it: "Some magic takes place in the crucible of leadership. . . . The individual brings certain attributes into the crucible and emerges with new, improved leadership skills. Whatever is thrown at them, leaders emerge from their crucibles stronger and unbroken."

That's the arc. We're smacked in the head by the realization that life isn't unfolding as we'd hoped, that all our careful plotting hasn't protected us from the shock of failure and disappointment. Our lives falter. Our companies stagger. We are in that alchemist's crucible, and the heat of loss and pain is turned up. We're being cooked.

Our co-founder has quit. Our investors pull funding. Our number one customer returns the product because it simply doesn't work. Our spouse gives up on us. Our board fires us. Such are the moments to stare deeply into our own experience. Who are we? What are we made of? What conditions are our lives in and, radically as important, how have we been complicit in creating the conditions we so steadfastly declare we do not want?

From that place, the warrior leader emerges.

I stare at this gentle but fierce, caring but incisive man and realize that he has emerged not only as the CEO he was meant to be but as a man stronger and unbroken. His resiliency rises from the very same place that holds his pain. His loss is the source of his strength.

Who knew that his truest, most demanding crucible of leadership, the moment of his fiercest emergence, would come at the end of his first turn in the CEO seat?

THE CRUCIBLE OF LEADERSHIP

Learning to lead yourself is the hardest part of becoming a leader. That's one of the things new CEOs and aspiring entrepreneurs come to me for. They come because they feel lonely; they don't have anyplace else to put the feelings. They'll sit on my couch or pace while they talk on the phone, pausing as we grapple with issue after issue after issue.

Learning to lead yourself is hard because we are wired to look outward. We feel pain and we look up and out to see who's hurt us. We feel loss, and the hurt gives rise to anger as we look for someone to blame.

Learning to lead yourself is hard because it requires us to look at the reality of all that we are—not to fix blame on ourselves but to understand with clarity what is really happening in our lives.

Learning to lead yourself is hard because it is painful. Growth is painful; that's why so few choose to do it.

Moreover, the common denominator in all our struggles is always people. When I first take on clients, I warn them that I don't have a magic wand. Nevertheless, their wish for some elixir to mend their relationships is heartbreakingly visceral.

When we start our leadership journey together, my clients frequently assume that the hardest part of their job will be figuring out what to do, what strategies to deploy, what business models to operationalize. Like so many, they have been seduced by the notion that being a leader means having all the answers, solving all the problems, and telling everyone else what to do.

Self-doubt convinces us that there's a magic path and if we can only find and follow the yellow-brick road, we'll end up safe, warm, and happy—successful leaders, beloved adults, retiring in Millionaire Acres at the end of The Game of Life. And we'll never be hungry, cold, alone, or afraid again.

One of the most profound teachings I've ever received came from a simple sutra from the Buddha: we are basically, unalterably good. We are born that way. (And, as evidence, the Buddha pointed to our humanity. Only humans, he taught, can achieve enlightenment and so, simply because we are human, we are essentially good.)

But each of us grows, seeking love, safety, and belonging. We seek to love and be loved. We need to feel safe physically, spiritually, and existentially. And we yearn to belong.

Learning to lead ourselves is hard because in the pursuit of love, safety, and belonging, we lose sight of our basic goodness and twist ourselves into what we think others want us to be. We move away from the source of our strengths—our core beliefs, the values we hold dear, the hard-earned wisdom of life—and toward an imagined playbook listing the right way to be.

We are inevitably knocked on our asses by the demands of leading. And when we make mistakes—when we fail to lead— our identity; our sense of self; our self-esteem; our deeply held beliefs about what it will take to feel loved and safe and that we belong, as well as that most the basic ability to provide for ourselves and our loved ones, seems to implode.

All too often we break down in the work of becoming a CEO, a manager, a leader. But in that breaking is the promise of a making.

I've seen it happen before. Take Steve Kane, for example, co-founder and former CEO of Gamesville. Back in the old days, in June 1999, when I was a venture capitalist and a partner to Fred Wilson in Flatiron Partners, we'd invested in Gamesville. The company was one of the fastest-growing gaming and entertainment sites around. More to the point, it was fun. (One of their bumper sticker logos: WASTING YOUR TIME SINCE 1996!)

A few months after we put a financial stake in the business, investment bankers began calling: "Let's take you public!"

Back then, any company with revenue could sell itself to the public capital markets, and the investors and founders could cash out. It was the thing to do then. What's more, Gamesville was going to be profitable. Hell, we were all going to be rich.

But then Lycos, Inc., came calling. Back then, BG—"before Google," as I like to put it—Lycos was one of the big search engines, and they were collecting sites and building out their portal business. They offered more than $230 million for Gamesville.

For Steve and his colleagues, it would mean they would be rich and would not have to be subject to the intense scrutiny and unrelenting criticism from public market investors who know little about your company and make money simply on the movement—up and down—of your stock price.

The board of directors wanted Steve to reject the deal. The collective sentiment was that the company would be better off going public. "Better off," defined as making everyone more money in the short term. Steve had his doubts.

"Jerry, my Dad worked his whole life building his company," I remember him telling me.

"He died, and I liquidated the company and gave my mother a check for a few million dollars. Taking this deal will mean millions to me and my family," he continued. "I'd be a fool to turn this down."

Years later Steve told me that he'd "had the great good fortune to learn a ton from working with a father who was an entrepreneur—though he never used that word."

"He was full of juicy, fun nuggets of wisdom," Steve said, "things like 'Never be ashamed to make a profit.' and 'The goal is to buy low and sell high, not buy lowest and sell highest.'"

Months later, when we would have been preparing to go public, the stock market crashed, and the door for IPOs slammed shut for companies like Gamesville. Steve had been lucky and prescient. He'd also followed his father's advice to focus on selling high, not at the highest, and the result was wonderful for him, his co-founders, and his investors. More to the point, Steve also become a leader in the process of deliberating over the company's future—and his own.

His crucible moment wasn't merely that he correctly foresaw that going public wasn't right for Gamesville. And it wasn't merely that he knew that a bird in his hand was worth more than the millions in the bush. It's that he had stayed in touch with where he was from and what had formed him. He remembered that he was the son of an entrepreneur, a scrappy, end-the-day-with-more-money-than-you-began entrepreneur. His dad and my iceman grandfather would have loved to play cards together.

Or consider Alex, one of the first CEOs in whom I invested back in the days of Flatiron Partners. Months after we closed our investment in his start-up, months after the company had been chugging along to build out the service that had been promised in the business plan, Alex called a board meeting.

"It's not going to work," he told the board two months before the launch. I was in shock. "What?" I asked myself, "How could he know this?"

"I just know," he said, as if to answer my silent question. He offered two choices: pull the plug on the business and return the remaining money to investors or let him fire everyone, except for his CFO, and give them a month to come back with a new plan. If we liked the plan, we'd use the remaining capital to fund the new business; if we didn't, we'd pull the plug then.

We chose the second path. This two-man operation relaunched the business, and two years later we sold the company for five times what we paid to invest.

Alex's crucible moment was the stark realization that the company wasn't going to work. I often think of Alex when I work with clients today. That start-up still had plenty of cash in the bank. The company still had investors who believed in its leadership. And it hadn't yet had customers failing to buy the service. But Alex had the presence of mind, the steadfastness, and the courage to confront reality.

That resolve to do what was right—to offer his investors the opportunity to back out and take back their money—enabled all of us to pull closer together and focus on executing a strategy that would work. Indeed, it was his courage and honesty that enabled our group to come together. That experience taught me something else about the crucible moment: when the leader moves through that moment, it enables those around them to grow as well.

I remember the moment in the board meeting when I realized what Alex was saying. I realized that the money I had just invested on behalf of my firm might be lost. But while Alex and the other board members were equally scared, they believed and trusted each other, having first come together in a previous company, also led by Alex. They believed in each other.

So, terrified that I was going to lose my firm's money, I, too, held myself steady.

I trusted in the honesty with which we faced the challenge.

Two years later we sold the company for a substantial return on investment. But I gained something more than cash. I received a powerful lesson in facing reality when something is failing, in trusting the team, and in holding oneself steady. I learned the power of the warrior pose.

The only answer, the only balm against the inevitable, existential pain of becoming the leaders we were born to be is to see the lessons implicit in the practice of *becoming*.

That's the true message of Warren Bennis's crucible. The magic, the alchemy, occurs when what we do mixes with who we are and is cooked by the heat of what we believe.

The Buddhists teach that for the steadfast warrior to emerge, we've got to break open our hearts to what is.

THE WARRIOR

"Stand up," I tell him. We are in Chad's office; the mini-fridge he keeps stocked with cans of seltzer is humming. His tiny cloth handmade KEEP ETSY WEIRD banner hangs from his handmade bookcase. His guitar rests in the handmade stand. I repeat myself: "Come on . . . I'm serious . . . stand up."

So, he stands, shoulders slumping. His sheepish grin tells me what's on his mind: "Oh, Jerry, now what are you going to make me do?" He trusts me, though, and he's used to me pushing him.

"Stand with your feet shoulder-width apart," I tell him. "Straighten up. Make your back firm but not tight." He complies. "Now drop your arms to your sides and turn your palms out, spreading your fingers." His slight swaying slows until his feet are in firm contact with the floor, the Earth.

"What do you feel?" I ask.

"Strong but . . ." he hesitates, "but also exposed."

Exactly so. Strong back and open heart. This is warrior stance, I tell him. The strong back of fiscal discipline. The strong back of clarity and vision, of drive and direction. The strong back of delegating responsibility and holding people accountable. The strong back of knowing right from wrong.

But it's also the open heart. It's giving a shit about people, purpose, meaning. It's working toward something greater than merely boosting your ego, greater than just soothing your worries and chasing your demons away. It's leading from within, drawing on the core of your being, on all that has shaped you.

Parker Palmer, whose grace, simplicity, and elegance have meant a great deal to me, likes to explain the concept of leading from within with a Hasidic tale he's taken from the philosopher Jacob Needleman:

A disciple asks the rabbi: "Why does Torah tell us to 'place these words *upon* your hearts'? Why does it not tell us to place these holy words *in* our hearts?" The Rabbi answers: "It is because as we are, our hearts are closed, and we cannot place the holy words in our hearts. So, we place them on top of our hearts. And there they stay until, one day, the heart breaks and the words fall in."

The warrior stance, I tell Chad, is the only true way to meet reality. The warrior stance creates the conditions in which our inner and outer begin to dance together. The warrior stance allows us to say, "Here I am, *mess and all*, do with me what you will." The toughest aspect of being a leader—hell, of being an adult—is meeting the world as it is and not as we wish it to be. The demons of the world, the demons of your soul, require just one thing: your broken-open heart.

EAT ME IF YOU WISH

There's a story told of Milarepa, the great Buddhist saint and teacher. It's said that one day he left his meditation cave to gather firewood. When he returned, the cave was filled with demons. I like to think of them as little bats, flying around the cave, making a nuisance of themselves.

Unsure of what to do, he begins to wave his arms at them, trying to get them to leave the cave so that he can go back to his meditations in peace. But they don't leave. Instead, they multiply. So, Milarepa becomes very clever. He says to himself, "I will teach them the dharma, the teachings of the Buddha." And the demons all quiet down and sit still. But Milarepa notices that, while the demons are quiet, they haven't left, and their number hasn't diminished.

Becoming slightly wiser and mildly more adult, he asks the demons, "What are you here to teach me?" One by one, the demons disappear.

Pleased with himself, Milarepa goes back to his meditation but realizes that one demon remains, a big, hairy bloodcurdling demon with big green eyes and bloody fangs. Shaking, terrified, Milarepa puts his head into the mouth of the demon and says, "Eat me if you wish." With that, the demon vanishes.

Surrendering to the demons that torment you and your organization doesn't mean abdicating your responsibilities to manage. You are still responsible for dealing with the reality of what is. You are still required to have the strong back, for example, of knowing when you're wrong.

In some cases, as at Alex's start-up, the demon is that you have the wrong vision for the company. In others, it may be that you've hired the wrong people. In still others, it may be your own failings—like an inability to admit that you're wrong.

But in all cases, allowing yourself to be eaten by the demon that remains—acknowledging how you have contributed to the problem without descending into pointless self-flagellation—turns up the heat beneath the crucible. Without heat, there is no alchemy.

I remember one client, a CEO. Both she and a co-founder had a host of physical ailments—migraines and stomach problems. More to the point, they'd both argued relentlessly with each other. The arguments had gotten so bad that neither could stand to be in the same room with the other. Even I was exasperated. During one late-night call, I asked my client to forget, for a moment, whether her co-founder was right or wrong. "I don't care who's right," I yelled in frustration. "The only thing we have to focus on is what are you supposed to be learning from this."

There was a long silence. I thought, "Okay. You've really pushed her too far. You and your woo-woo 'lessons in the pain' crap." But then: alchemy. She opened up and put her head into the mouth of the demon.

"This is really shameful to admit," she began, "but I know I'm a pain in the ass, because I have to be right, all the time. I know it's wrong, but I can't stop myself."

With that, we had something to work with. I pressed her: Given this tendency, what do you really believe? What values do you hold? What kind of company do you want to build? And what kind of adult do you want to be?

"Why?" I asked inelegantly and in a very uncoachlike way. "Why do you need to be right?"

She released a deep breath, a sigh, "Because if I was wrong, my Dad would wipe me out." And the tears flowed, and the sobs took even my breath away. "I was never sure I was safe. I had to prove myself worthy every night. He would grill me over dinner about my day and the choices I had made. I learned early on that the only way to survive was to be right."

Over the next few weeks, on guard for her need to be right, we carefully went to work changing her approach to the co-founder. For her, the crucible moment came in facing her shame, acknowledging who she really had been. As a result, she got to choose how she wanted to manage, what kind of company she wanted to work for, and who she wanted to be as a leader.

We forge our truest identity by putting our heads into the mouths of the scariest demons, the realities of our lives. Only by facing our fears, our prejudices, our passions, can we transform the energy that is the source of our aggression, the source of our confusion, the source of our struggle.

When I was a young man, I'd often lament to Dr. Sayres about my own fears as a manager. After a series of infuriating questions, she got me to admit that I was trapped by my own beliefs about success. Then came the admission that I would never be satisfied until I was as successful as Bill Gates.

So many young leaders struggle with the tendency to compare themselves, often unflatteringly, to better-known leaders—leaders such as Bill Gates or, even and despite his controversial character, Steve Jobs.

Years ago, Joel Spolsky, the co-founder of companies such as Fog Creek Software, Trello, and Stack Exchange, took the "Steve Jobs Question" head-on:

"And yes, you're right," he once wrote, Steve Jobs created one of the most successful companies in the history of humanity and he ". . . was a dictatorial, autocratic asshole who ruled by fiat and fear." But, importantly, he pointed out "you are not Steve Jobs." Meaning, you are not as bright as Steve was. More important, though, you don't have to be like Steve to succeed.

I wasn't and—importantly, had no need to be—Bill Gates. Indeed, I often think of the teaching of Jesus. It's a lesser-known teaching from the one of the Gnostic Gospels, the Gospel of Saint Thomas:

"If you bring forth what is in you, what is in you will save you. If you do not bring forth what is in you, what is in you will destroy you."

Jesus taught a truth: the only choice that doesn't destroy you is to bring forth who you were meant to be. The alchemy of becoming yourself is the ultimate magic act and fullest expression of leadership.

In all these thoughts I read a steady, consistent wisdom: the wisdom of knowing yourself and your own beliefs and living them. Enduring the alchemical crucible requires developing the capacity to reflect, to turn the pain of the everyday life as a leader into lessons. Every wisdom tradition I've ever encountered demands the same thing: we must go inward.

As my friend the poet Pádraig Ó Tuama would say, "Hello to knowing the story of yourself."

That's often the biggest obstacle to becoming yourself. The frenzied, frenetic, "do it now, answer the e-mail now or the company will die, even though it's three a.m." attitude is precisely the wrong process of becoming yourself.

BROKENHEARTED WARRIORS LEAD BEST

Back on the roof, Chad and I talk of life, love, and loss; the inevitable, painful path of change; the impermanence of all things. The story of my friend Chad is a story of movement, of change. It's the story of a boy, a native son of North Carolina, a scholarship recipient at Duke University, a true Tar Heel, who grew up to be the CEO of a multibillion-dollar company. And grow up he did. It's the story of man whose loss of status has made possible the claiming of something even greater: his truest self.

That's the greatest crucible of all: Learning to bring forth not only what is *in* you but the *whole* of you, the glory of you as well as the mess of you. Taking your seat, putting your head into the mouth of all the demons of your life and challenging them to eat you if they wish. Taking these steps allows you to take on more than your leadership; it allows you to sit like royalty, like someone who belongs at the table, deserving of having become the person you were always meant to be.

Hello to humans who occupy the fullness—the glory *and* the mess—of their lives. Hello to broken-open-hearted warriors. Hello to the leaders this broken world needs most. Hello to being the leader you were born to be. Hello to warriors with broken-open hearts.

There is no one way, but there is one requirement: to go inward. Sitting still, hanging out in the spaces between the frames of life speeding by: that is the path to radical self-inquiry.

Journaling Invitations

How can I lead with the dignity, courage,
and grace that are my birthright?

———

How can I use even the loss of status and the
challenge to my self-esteem inherent in leadership
to grow into the adult I want to be in the world?

———

At the end of my tenure in my current position,
what would I like to feel about myself?

———

CHAPTER 3

Standing Still in Empty Time

I know what it's like to be lost. I know what it's like to be found. I want to tell you how to recognize when you're lost. I want you to know how to be found. I want to tell you how I learned to stand still so that you, too, can learn to stand still. The poet David Wagoner writes: "The forest knows / Where you are. You must let it find you."

To let the forest find you, he says, you've got to stand still.

I ended my teen years in the locked psych ward of Cabrini Hospital in Manhattan. There are two kinds of psych wards: locked and unlocked. Those who spend time in a locked ward are considered a danger, either to themselves or to others. Being on the inside of locked is dreadful. I'll never forget the click of the lock falling into place as my friends and family, visitors, would leave me behind.

The pain, terror, and dislocating confusion of my childhood had left me feeling that I'd had no other options. I was journaling then but didn't have a voice. I could only sputter an incomplete and inchoate description of what was going on in my heart.

Shortly after my eighteenth birthday—on January 2, 1982, sitting at my desk in a bedroom in a home in Ozone Park, Queens, a home my father had inherited from his parents, a building they'd purchased in the 1920s, a home in which I and some, but not all, of my siblings lived with our parents—I used an X-Acto knife to trace lines across my wrists, back and forth, back and forth, until the skin on each side of the line I'd traced separated and first tiny drops and then a river of blood appeared.

A night in the emergency room at Jamaica Hospital was followed by a mandatory three days in Creedmoor State Hospital, in a locked room where a burly West Indian attendant stood watch over me—I was on suicide watch. This was followed by a three-month stay at Cabrini Hospital, behind another locked door.

One of the ways I'd coped with my childhood and teen years was by *doing*. I perfected the art of doing. I was busy—always *busy*. In addition to doing well academically through most of my school years, I was *involved*. I was involved in plays, student government, local politics. When I ran out of things to do, I'd take on more commitments.

The most familiar bodily sensations of my childhood, those that didn't involve my being teased and bullied by siblings or kids such as Pablo, were those of my heart racing and beads of sweat running down my temples.

When I left Cabrini, I took up where I'd left off and began *doing* again. I'd moved out of my parents' house and into my sister Mary's place. I got a job as, first, a busboy and then as a waiter and worked late into the night. I went back to school, Queens College, that September. While I was supported financially—for example, despite her own constraints, my sister Mary sent me fifteen dollars a week so that I could pay for therapy—I was on my own; ending my teen years early, I promoted myself into manhood.

I was behind in my classes, so I doubled up, taking more than the usual share of credits. What's more, despite the incredibly cheap tuition of, I recall, $750 a semester, I never had enough money. I took first one job, then another, and then still another. I spent the next few years in constant motion. Therapy, subway rides, classes, and work dominated my life.

Looking back, I see all those subway rides, all that motion, as an attempt to gather lemon drops. My twisted logic went like this: I didn't have any lemon drops, and therefore felt exhausted and depleted and constantly battled migraines, because I wasn't doing enough. The answer, therefore, was simple: Do more, faster.

I raced through my days. From class, to therapy, to work, to class. The bus to the train to the bus to the train. Sometimes the only sleep I'd snatch was on the grass on the quad on campus, a pleasant place to rest, or in the art library (not the regular library, that was too noisy). Beads of sweat flowed down my temples and the back of my neck.

My meals consisted mostly of oatmeal; it was cheap and

temporarily sated hunger. I'd fill a large thermos with Quaker Instant Oatmeal and eat that all day long.

One night, after a fourteen-hour day that included ninety-minute subway rides to and from the Queens College campus, I collapsed onto my mattress in the makeshift bedroom I'd created in the dining room of the apartment I shared with my brother Dominic. I lay there, sweating, gasping, shaking.

I'd fallen asleep in the clothes I'd worn the day before. I woke a few hours later to the sounds of violence, as the bookshelves I'd installed as a makeshift closet in my makeshift bedroom ripped out of the wall and everything I owned tumbled down on top of me. I lay there, covered in jeans, underwear, T-shirts, and twisted metal shelving.

Breathless, Dominic came rushing in: "Are you all right?"

"Yes," I mumbled, and went back to sleep, not even bothering to throw off the piles that had rained down on me.

A few months later, I found myself desperate and anxious. The spring semester had started, and I had been dodging notices from the bursar's office. Weeks into the semester, I still hadn't paid my tuition; I couldn't scrape together the $750.

Robert Greenberg was my favorite professor. His love of poetry, especially that of the Romantics, fueled my earliest love of poetry. Looking every bit the academic, he sported a close-cropped gray beard and wore small, round glasses beneath his balding head. I can still hear him quoting from William Blake's "The Chimney Sweeper":

And my father sold me while yet my tongue
Could scarcely cry "'weep! 'weep! 'weep! 'weep!"

Professor Greenberg was also my adviser. One day, with the weight of the unpaid tuition bearing down on me, I confessed to him that I'd be leaving school. I couldn't pay my tuition. I weep now as I remember his reaction: "Well, that's not going to happen." He paused, wiping his glasses slowly and then putting them back on. "You've just won a scholarship that will pay your tuition until you graduate."

He explained that he was the only judge in a competition and had decided just then that he couldn't think of a more deserving student.

The scholarship was given by a small publishing company on Long Island. CMP Media had been founded by a husband-and-wife team, Gerry and Lilo Leeds. Lilo, who was Jewish, had grown up in Germany in the 1930s and left before the Nazis turned the country into a hell. She went to Queens College and established the scholarship. I was the first recipient.

At the meeting with her in the president's office to pick up the scholarship check and take photos for the school newspaper, I fast-talked my way into an internship for the summer.

I began working at *InformationWeek*, a weekly newsmagazine covering technology and business. By the end of the summer, despite the fact that I knew nothing about technology or business, I fast-talked my way, again, into a part-time job as a reporter.

Two years later, having taught myself a few things about technology and business, I finished school and became a full-time reporter. Two years after that, having taught myself a few things about leading and managing, I was promoted first to news editor and then to editor of the magazine.

When I was twenty-one, I had lain under a pile of worn-out clothes, waiflike and malnourished. Four years later, at the age of twenty-five, I was the editor of a magazine with four hundred thousand readers and a staff of forty.

The next few years were even more of a blur. No. Not a blur because of memory or the passage of time. They were a blur because motion was followed by more motion, beads of sweat were followed by more beads of sweat.

I still hadn't acquired *enough* to begin to feel safe, but at least I was eating more than oatmeal. Looking back now, I remember that time as one in which I seemed to barely occupy my body. But that realization came later—much later—when I came to understand that one of the by-products of standing still is to fully occupy the meat bag that is your body.

I still remember the feeling of moving through work as if I were the Marvel superhero the Flash. I'd race from floor to floor, meeting to meeting, imagining that my cheeks were blown back and puffed out, as in the pictures of those guys in the 1960s who'd broken the land-speed records. I still remember watching my colleagues moving slowly, as if they were underwater. Even now, my heart still races at the thought of closing the last form, the last eight pages of the magazine, on Friday morning, when we'd scramble to fit in the latest-breaking news.

I know now that, despite what my frantic mind told me then, the constant motion wasn't a requirement of the job I'd chosen. But producing a weekly magazine with daily deadlines was the perfect job for someone who mistook motion for meaning. Everyone thought I was thriving but, on the inside, I was dying.

The non-occupation of my body was obvious to those who cared to look closely. I was busy, I was alert and active, but I wasn't really present in my life. My eyes darting from one person to another, listening without hearing—I wasn't really attending to my life, and I wasn't really connecting to the people who mattered most to me.

In so many ways, the world affirmed this way of being. I was rewarded with promotions. Years later, and with the benefit of thousands of hours of introspection, I understand why the world affirmed this way of being. When I moved fast, when I spent my days not truly occupying my life, not standing still, not being real, I found it easier to live in accordance with other people's expectations. By not standing still, I was able to be the object of everyone else's projections of who and what I should be. Too busy to live my own life, I took direction from the affirmations of others.

Since the world needed an editorial wunderkind to direct a magazine about technology, I'd readily put aside my love of writing and poetry and took on the mantle of being a technologist. My family, I thought, needed someone who was happy, smart, and capable, and I donned the cape of the good student, the fast-rising executive, who was also everyone's friend.

But this act deafened me to my own voice and numbed me to the urges of my own body—for sleep, for recovery, for love, for the poetry that soothes my soul.

The world loved my doing. But the more the world applauded,

the more my soul ached. "My soul was a burden, bruised, and bleeding," wrote Saint Augustine, "It was tired of the man who carried it." I was growing tired of carrying my soul.

This strategy of moving quickly was not unlike another survival strategy I had developed as a child, my hyperawareness of the Other's sense of being. As a boy, I could discern Dad's mood by the way he walked down the hallway to our ground-floor apartment. If he shuffled, I knew he was slightly drunk; if his shoes clicked on the hallway linoleum, then he hadn't stopped at a bar on the way home from work. On a good night, I could make it to bed before he was drunk.

Indeed, I was always on guard. I'd listen and watch my parents with great intensity. As Dad worked his way through his nightly Pabst Blue Ribbons, his words became looser, his enunciation less clipped. If I was unfortunate enough to be awake before he started his second six-pack of beer, I could feel the tension in my mother build. She hated his drinking, and he drank every night.

The indications of her mounting duress were less visible but no less visceral. She'd light a cigarette and begin moving about the kitchen, picking up and then just as briskly putting down objects: ashtrays, glasses, the little replica of Christ's crucifixion my brother Dominic had made; anything, really, she touched. The ritual movement—snatch it up, move it slightly, put it down—would slowly spread and deepen in intensity until it felt as if, with each putting-down, my whole world was nearing implosion.

Often, suddenly, an ashtray would be slammed down, and Mom would begin muttering first under her breath and then louder and louder, speaking to everyone and to no one in particular. No one, that is, that might be in the room.

Some nights it was Jesus. Some nights it was the late Bobby Kennedy—maybe even Art Garfunkel.

As *Gunsmoke* or Mutual of Omaha's *Wild Kingdom* played on the black-and-white TV, my ears would prick up, scanning for the threat. As the words flowed, and as the night promised to pass in another endless torrent of words, the rest of us, sometimes all seven of us kids, would tighten, go silent, cower slightly, each pretending to just watch the cheetah eat an antelope or Sheriff Matt Dillon capture the bandit without shooting him.

The worst storms were those when Dad engaged Mom, answering her comments about his infidelities, his drinking, his having been given up at birth to be adopted by Grandma and Grandpa Colonna.

Over time, hyperawareness became part of my character, part of me. It became, as I've often joked, a superpower. Even today, when I work with coaching clients, I track every bob of the Adam's apple, every pause in the story (where it occurs, what words preceded and followed it, where their eyes move when they pause), to brace for the coming storm or, even more, to discern what they might need, right then, in that moment. If I give them what they need, says my little boy, they will be saved, and if I've saved them, then I'll be safe.

That hyperawareness, married to the quick-change nature of my presentation of self, gave me the ability to meet everyone's expectations of who I should be.

My propensity for speed and busyness and my ability to

read others were matched by an insatiable curiosity. I read constantly. I devoured books, ideas, and information. And I asked questions, lots of questions.

Even today, the questions I ask can be unsettling. When used well, people on the other side of the question can feel an uncanny and unexpected sense of being truly seen. When not used well, they can feel like they're facing an inquisition, with my hypervigilance creeping back up and threatening to break the fragile connection between us.

These traits—insatiable curiosity, a driving need for speed, the ability to read people, and the ability to anticipate problems before they arise—led others to view me as a rising star, a wunderkind. Quite a transition for a guy who, only a few years before, had been a psych patient in a locked ward.

And yet, even as I progressed in my career, the beads-of-sweat years continued.

MY RADICAL SELF-INQUIRY

As 1994 began, I left CMP, left journalism, and helped form a venture capital firm, CMG@Ventures. At CMG, we were among the first firms to focus specifically on opportunities emerging from the newly developed World Wide Web.

Leaving the media business only intensified those beads-of-sweat years.

Two years later, I was on the move again. I left CMG@ Ventures to form a new venture capital firm with Fred Wilson. On the surface, Fred's ten years' experience as a venture capitalist (VC) and a Wharton MBA made him the perfect partner for me, a guy who could barely read a profit-and-loss statement. But, more to the point, we both cared as much about how something was done as we did about the outcome.

Flatiron Partners was founded in June 1996, and the media quickly hailed us for creating a technology-focused venture capital firm based in New York City. We weren't the first. And we hadn't made any investments, so no one could tell whether we'd be any good. But the press loved the story, and we were on the front page of the business section of the *New York Times* and several other financial outlets.

A few weeks after officially launching Flatiron Partners, I was walking on the beach with my kids. Seagulls darted and wheeled through the sky, the birds' cries mixing with the sounds of the surf pounding the shore. We walked through a tunnel under the boardwalk, in search of a bathroom and ice cream. Stepping into the cool dark, I felt relief from the face-melting sun. Stepping back into the light, I was struck to my knees by a blinding pain that ripped across my skull.

I fell to the ground, writhing.

I drifted in and out of consciousness and came to in an emergency room. No one could make sense of the headache that had ripped through my skull. A spinal tap was performed, bringing with it a fresh round of nausea.

After a week in the hospital and a battery of tests, the neurologist concluded, "Probably cluster headaches." *Probably*, he said, but he could find nothing physically wrong with me. Fred, my business partner, raised a proper Catholic, with innumerable ways to feel guilt, was convinced that, because of the timing of the headache—one week after we had announced the formation of Flatiron, it was his fault. My then-therapist Dr. Sayres had other ideas.

I sensed that she'd grown frustrated by my frequent headaches. It wasn't uncommon for me to be woken from a deep sleep with a skull-splitting headache, for example.

Following that incident, she began helping me connect the dots between my waking-world stresses from things such as the busyness, the hyperawareness, and my propensity to shape-shift to fit the scene, often withholding even from myself my most deeply held feelings. In those weeks, she began pushing me to ask myself one simple question: "What am I not saying that needs to be said?"

Looking back, I realize this time as the beginning of my own radical self-inquiry. My pain helped me realize that I was lost. My soul, no longer content to be "bruised and battered," took charge of my body and grabbed the attention of my conscious mind. The headaches, which continued even as the self-inquiry began, became a way for my body to say, in effect, "Wake the fuck up."

For, if I didn't wake up, my soul was going to drop me to my knees, writhing in pain.

In therapy with Dr. Sayres, we unpacked the months preceding the vomit-inducing cluster headaches. I was in a job I couldn't stand. I was working with people I couldn't trust. I was living a life that was not my own. I was living, as Parker Palmer would describe, "divided," where the inner me didn't match the outer me. I was just thirty but already the years of living life at a beads-of-sweat pace, of moving forward even though I was lost, were exacting their price. But I was obstinate and thick-headed. The lesson that began on the beach that day took years to sink in. I put on my superhero cape once again and doubled down on my strategy.

Flatiron Partners unfolded in glorious ways. For years we were celebrated, feted. Part of that feting seems warranted; from all appearances, it seemed we could do no wrong. Every investment made money. But the accolades we received as a firm felt a bit like the affirmations I'd received as a rising star—false in that they were based not on our values, our shared sense of purpose, but on the whimsy of whether we were making money.

If there was a conversation about the emerging technology scene in New York, we were called. Sometimes we were chastised as part of all that was wrong with the growing fascination with all things Internet.

Nevertheless, I continued to move fast and do more. I vividly recall coming off the elevator and heading into the office and panting in anticipation and fear of what might be coming at me from around the next corner.

"IF I'M NOT PANTING, I FEEL LIKE I'M NOT WORKING."

Years later, I'm coaching Victor; his shoulders are hunched, and he's leaning toward me. He's a potential new client, the co-founder of a struggling start-up trying to compete in a new but already crowded market. He's come to me in confusion and looking for answers. All I have for him are questions: "What are you not saying that needs to be said?"

He's got dark eyes, thick eyebrows, and a full beard. At twenty-five, he's the same age I was when I took over the magazine at CMP.

"Well, I'm worried about the money," I remember him telling me. "I mean this first conversation has made me feel great but is it, I don't know, 'justifiable' to spend the company's money on making the CEO feel better?"

"How much can you spend so that it feels justified?"

"I don't know," he stammers, his thick Adam's apple bobbing, "Seventy-five dollars?"

"Sold," I say with a smile.

He starts to cry. "What? What is it?" I ask.

"I don't feel worthy."

Victor is an immigrant. He grew up during his country's civil war. He spent most of the years of that war in bed being treated for cancer. The wounds from the cancer are in his body, still, but in his soul as well; "I don't feel worthy."

Perhaps it was nothing but some general fear that made him question his worthiness. But, nevertheless, the combination of a devastatingly frightening war and a life-threatening illness left the boy with the only answer his mind could grasp: "I am not worthy."

We worked for a few years as he grew into his role as CEO. I watched as the young man became just a *man*—no qualifier needed. Toward the end of our time together we began working on his struggles to commit to something beyond work. There was a girl. They were in love. And they fought because she "never" saw him; he was always working.

"What is it?" I asked. "What's keeping you at your desk all

night? What stops you from, I don't know, just taking her to the movies?"

"I'm afraid!" he barked at me, as if it were obvious. "I'm afraid that if I don't work hard I'll end up back there."

"Back there" was his code phrase for the war and the cancer.

"I'm afraid," he continued, "that if I slow down . . ." He hesitated. "It's like this—if I'm not panting, I feel like I'm not working."

There it is. That same old haunting belief system. Run faster and faster, telling oneself that the way to be is to do; do more, faster, and just maybe you'll outrun war, cancer, and the other demons that cause you to doubt your worth, your lovability, and your own voice.

But panting through work is a lousy strategy. It feeds the anxiety of never enough; it gets in the way of thinking clearly; and it convinces you to mistake motion for meaning.

Recently I did an interview with a presenter from the BBC. He asked in that lovely, proper, obvious way unique to BBC presenters, "But isn't working hard just a part of the job?"

"Yes. Of course," I replied. "But that's not what we're talking about. Tell me the brilliant ideas, the innovations that move an organization—a community of people—forward that spring from panic and fear."

When you use your position, power, agency and the resources of a company; when you unconsciously bend colleagues, friends, and family to serve your hunger for love, safety, and a sense of belonging—oh, those longed-for lemon drops—you stand in the way of finding a mission that unites everyone in the first place.

You're not leading when you spend your time trying to out-run your demons, trying to numb yourself to the hungers that come from within.

I understand the impulse. It's a rush to, well, *rush* from task to task. Moreover, it feeds a sense of superiority: "Geez, my work must be so important . . . look how fast I'm moving!"

But it can also feed distrust and disunity; "Look how fast I'm moving," when said by one who holds power, implies a profoundly disheartening and negative statement: "Look at how slowly you're moving."

A deeper look shows that the view is also fed by a tendency to merge what we do with who we are. "We are nothing," we tell ourselves, "unless we are doing." Our value as humans becomes dependent on whether we've gotten the A in the class, raised the funds our nascent start-up needs, gotten the right accolades from those above us, married the right partner, purchased the right home. I am what I do, and if what I'm doing is fast and, therefore, important, then I must be worthy enough to have earned your respect, your love. And if not your love, then maybe—just maybe—the love of my parents.

While everyone—myself included—can fall prey to using work as a prop for self-meaning, founders are particularly susceptible to this loss of self. Think of the many, many jerks in business whom we admire precisely because they have a single-minded focus on execution, causing everyone around them to pant their way through the workday.

Of course, we don't put it that way. We admire them because they are successful—their means are justified by their accomplishments. The lure of losing oneself in work is immensely seductive. What's more, great and impossible things are often achieved through this kind of merging of self with a larger purpose. Yes, yes, yes, there is a power in reaching for that larger-than-the-self purpose; "Ah, but a man's reach should exceed his grasp," wrote the poet Robert Browning, "or what's a heaven for?"

There's audacity in reaching, in dreaming of a new way to change a lightbulb, to search for something on the Internet, to connect people across time and space. That audacious reach should never be withheld.

But to lose one's footing in the reaching serves no one, especially not the one doing the reaching. It's a lousy way to live.

In the fall of 2010, I stepped on a subway at the Forty-Second Street station, Times Square. It was the uptown 1 train. I felt myself shoved and looked up, angry and startled. This was no ordinary jostle.

The next thing I remember, I was lying on my back, my head cradled in the lap of a cop, my body covered in blood. Coldcocked. Without provocation, without warning, I'd been knocked unconscious, the soft tissue of my nose damaged, my cheek lacerated, and one tooth broken. I couldn't remember my name, where I was headed, or who the president was. Lying on a gurney at Bellevue, I was struck by the realization that disappearing into the motion of life, losing touch with those inner worlds that define true success, is a really lousy way to live. It was as if the promise I had made to myself at eighteen, in the hospital after the suicide attempt—a promise to live fully—had merged with the fears of my childhood. I had created a life that was superficially rewarding but slowly killing me.

On the surface, I was thriving during what poet John Donohue would call my "empty-time" life. The gifts of this hollow time included fame and fortune. I had gone from covering the news to being news. This period had begun to feel like the crucial stage of the most important Monopoly game of my life. Look how I had surprised everyone, what with my neatly stacked bills and a hidden pile of money. How could I possibly quit now?

The world affirmed me for my willingness, my compulsion, to give more and more, to do more and more. But the more I gave, the more I lost. The more I lost, the closer I came to the lip of the stinking, belching hole in the ground known as Ground Zero.

WHAT NEEDS TO BE SAID

I don't remember the weather, but I can guarantee you that, to me, February 2002 felt dark, dank, and cold. I told my business partners that I was taking a vacation and, following my therapist's advice, booked two weeks at Canyon Ranch in Arizona. More important, though, I began opening to the folks in my life.

So much of that time remains indistinct, but I remember the two books my sister, Annie, recommended to me: Pema Chödrön's *When Things Fall Apart* and Parker's *Let Your Life Speak*. Both books, as well as Sharon Salzberg's *Faith*, flew with me to Arizona from New York.

I spent my time at Canyon Ranch reading, learning about meditation, and weeping. I began to learn the importance of *standing still*. Still enough to begin asking myself that question: What are you not saying that needs to be said?

Annie's simple gesture, two books with the loving embrace of a big sister, altered the trajectory of my life. Those books introduced me to two profoundly important concepts. *Let Your Life Speak* showed me that I was not speaking to, about, or from *my* life but the life of another. *When Things Fall Apart* helped me see that things are always falling apart; always. To expect otherwise is to invite suffering. Pema taught me that we must lean into the suffering and befriend it. Doing that requires just one thing: the courage to be still.

When he was a boy, my son Sam loved Maurice Sendak's *Where the Wild Things Are*, just as I had as a boy. Sam would listen intensely as I read of Max's adventures sailing to the wild things.

Our favorite part was just before the wild things crowned Max king.

I read, "And when he came to the place where the wild things are, they roared their terrible roars and gnashed their terrible teeth and rolled their terrible eyes and showed their terrible claws," roaring *my* terrible roars, rolling *my* terrible eyes, and showing *my* terrible claws, and then, when the passage came to Max yelling at the wild things, Sam would hold up his hand, like a cop stopping traffic, and would say Max's famous line: "Be still."

When I think of standing still in empty time, it helps to think of Sam; "Be still." Sendak's Max and my Sam both knew how to be with Wild Things. The only way to tame the monsters, the demons with their terrible roars and terrible claws, is to be still. This is the first step to radical self-inquiry; it starts with the courage to be still in the face of uncertainty.

In the months between my personal Ground Zero, my first encounters with Buddhist thinking, meditation, and—from Parker—the experience of a man, an elder, speaking openly about his struggles, I started to regain my life. Intrigued by these notions, I began to reboot my life. I told my business partners I had no intention of renewing my contract.

That first phase of my life reboot was easier than I had anticipated, but my partners' response was telling. One asked, after I told him that I had no idea what I was going to do next but that I was looking forward to life without a title or a business card, "What if no one calls you?"

I didn't have the courage then that I have now. Today I would respond, "That'd be wonderful." But at the time, my willingness to stand in the uncertainty, the impermanence of everything, was still new. The year following Ground Zero was punctuated by my deepening exploration. I began a four-year buying spree on Amazon. If it had to do with Buddhism, self-introspection, or existential crises, I read it.

But I was still merely a nightstand Buddhist. I had read a lot of books but hadn't really leaned into them. A few months later, I attended a hip fund-raiser hosted by two legendary downtown musicians; it was a benefit for a local Buddhist center and the beginning of a weekend teaching retreat led by

Pema Chödrön. Pema, with a wide grin on her shaved head, settled into a cushion in the middle of the room, the teacher's seat. She immediately started teaching on the nature of things falling apart. It's not just the material world, she noted. All things. All. Things. Our wishes, our dreams, our conceptions of who and what we are supposed to be, our sense of self, our sadness, our joy . . . all of it. Falling apart. All the time. Right before our eyes.

And that hurts. It hurts because the ego, the fragile persona we develop to combat the slings and arrows of outrageous fortune and our sense of utter unworthiness, believes that only by keeping things exactly as they are, moment to moment, can we be free of suffering.

I nodded knowingly; I knew how to be a good student. "Yes," I remember telling myself, "I read about this." Good boy, I said to myself.

Then, Pema did that thing Buddhist teachers are famous for doing. She delivered the coup de grâce, a whack upside my overconceptualizing head.

"Now," she began with a mischievous smile, "some of you are sitting there thinking: 'I got this. I understand this.'"

I squirmed.

"But even your understanding of this concept is falling apart all the time."

I blurted out, "That's not fair!"

I had just gotten this concept, I remember feeling, and you're telling me that I can't even hold on to getting it? She turned a twinkly eye to me and said knowingly, "Catholic, right?" She'd nailed me. Once again, I'd wanted nothing more than to be told how to get an A. How to get *it* right. This time, though, the *it* was feeling better.

Later we were each given time alone with Pema. With my heart beating fast and beginning to break open in ways it had never opened before, I knelt before her, the first American to be ordained a Tibetan Buddhist nun.

I blubbered and stammered. The ground had just been ripped from under me, and I was falling. I tried to explain what was happening to me and Pema, or "Ani" Pema, using her honorific title for nun, just smiled, tapped my hand lightly, lovingly and said, "Honey, whatever it is, you're not opening to it. You think you're open. But you're not. You need to keep opening." Looking back, I see now just how terribly lost I was. But I also see that I was beginning to find my way, beginning to let the forest find me.

Keep opening. Stand still. Keep opening and stand still. Open up, get curious, and inquire within.

Years later, after I'd begun coaching, I came across another teaching by Ani Pema in a tiny book called *How to Meditate.* In it, she refers to meditation as the act of stripping away delusion and being with what is, simply and wholly. That teaching came to mind when I was working with a client.

"Stop the spinning," I'd blurted out in utter frustration and nearly yelling. "Stop pitching me. Stop telling me you're crushing it, you're killing it, and that you've got it all figured out." I went on: "If you had it all figured out you wouldn't be sitting on my couch. Sit still and ask yourself why things are the way they are and why they aren't the way you'd like them to be."

There it was: radical self-inquiry. The process by which self-deception becomes so skillfully and *compassionately* exposed that no mask can hide us anymore. Radical in that such inquiry is rare. Radical in that it demands that we stop blaming others for our lives. Compassionate in the way a good teacher is compassionate: stop bullshitting yourself.

Slow down. Stand still. Breathe. Let the forest find you. Then you can begin to ask yourself the hardest questions: Who am I? What do I believe about the world? What do success and failure mean to me (and not to everyone else)? What kind of adult do I want to be? And, most helpful, how have I been complicit in creating the conditions in my life that I say I don't want?

CREATING A PLACE OF BELONGING

All the folks who come to our company's leadership boot camps complete applications in which they are encouraged to define with skill, compassion, and radical self-inquiry the things with which they struggle. Tracy Lawrence's application broke my heart. I remember her writing about her wish that the people at Chewse, the company she cofounded and where she serves as CEO, could be "just like software."

She wanted people to be knowable, predictable. She wanted some semblance of a guarantee that if the data that had been input were correct, the output would be effective. In 2016, in a podcast conversation in which we recalled that time, she and I spoke of her big breakthrough. A breakthrough that came about only because of her willingness to enter a different time, to stand still despite feeling as if her hair were on fire, to take a few days and think about her leadership and her life.

At the camp, we spoke about the ways our pasts shape our presents. We slowed down; we stood still; we dropped the bull-shitting, spinning, and the efforts to outrun the wild things. We inquired within. Looking puzzled, Tracy struggled to understand how her childhood was present in her adulthood.

"Tell me about shame," I answered her. Scrunching up her face, searching, her eyes suddenly got very wide. Her body small and still.

"What do you remember?" I asked.

"I was in middle school," she said in a dreamy reverie. She was teased relentlessly for having "different" hair. A mixed-race kid, her features weren't precisely like everyone else's.

"What happened?" I continued, the group joining us in the stillness.

"I spent the entire year eating my lunch in a bathroom stall to avoid the kids who were making fun of me." Lunch, for Tracy, meant humiliation, sadness, and pain; and the only way to be safe was to be alone. She wept as she remembered that time. She sobbed as she reentered those feelings. She sat still and felt the past wash over her.

"Tracy," I said, calling her back to the present. "Tracy, what does your company do?" Wiping her nose, she looked puzzled. "Tracy, tell me what Chewse does, what's its mission?"

"We provide nutritious lunches and snacks to other start-up companies," she answered really puzzled.

"And why is that important?" I asked.

Smiling and laughing, she replied, "So that people can get out from behind their desks and gather together for lunch . . . so that lunch isn't painful but loving. So that no one needs to eat alone to feel safe."

Her laugh that followed her realization shook the room with power and grace. In the transition from middle-schooler to adult, from child to start-up founder, Tracy had buried the memories of those taunts behind a wall of shame, glimpsed only occasionally.

But, unknown to her conscious mind, she had also transformed that time of enormous pain and self-loathing into a deeply held purpose. She was, of course, providing nutritious meals to folks at other start-up companies—her peers if not her friends. But she was also giving them an opportunity to belong—something denied her by the middle-school bullies of her past.

She reached into a dark, shame-filled place in her past and pulled from it a power: the power to belong.

What's more, by stilling her *wild things* (who danced in the moonlight of her memory telling her again and again that she didn't belong), she saw that her unconscious had given a way to transform that pain into a purpose.

In the months that followed that realization she changed the company's mission statement to include the word *love* and added a heart to the logo. She embraced the painful roots of her company's founding, realizing that Chewse wasn't merely an attempt to "disrupt the food delivery business" but an opportunity to give others what she herself had lacked: community.

Chewse then moved closer to a start-up's holy grail, profitability, and closed its largest round of financing. But, most important, Tracy no longer wonders why she cares so much about the business succeeding, why she worries so much about failure. She understands her sacred mission and, therefore, her core as a leader.

When you learn to stand still in lost and empty times, then the forest can find you and, what's more, you can find yourself.

Journaling Invitations

In what ways do I deplete myself and
run myself into the ground?

———————

Where am I running from and where to?

———————

Why have I allowed myself to be so exhausted?

———————

CHAPTER 4

Remembering Who You Are

It was the first night of one of our CEO boot camps. We were in Colorado; the aspens were golden under a bluish-black night. We were in a circle, establishing the safety of this community that, over the next few days, would come together, stand still, and begin the process of remembering who they were—the *whys* behind their life choices.

"The bullshitting stops here," I said, staring each of them in the eye. "No more spinning. No more lying." As I spoke, I could feel their bodies tense, contract in fear, and then relax as they let go and realized that I meant it. "No more feeding your delusional thoughts about how you're crushing it . . . how you've got it all figured it out." I paced the room like the preachers I so admire. "No more . . . because it only feeds that whispery voice in your head telling you again and again that you're an impostor."

The next morning, we again met in a circle and then sent campers off on a walk with a partner, someone they hadn't known before coming to the camp. We asked each pair to speak to each other about a single topic: "What I wish my colleagues knew about me is . . ."

The pairs returned from their walk more awake, more alive—energized by the connections they'd formed. We asked them to speak to the circle and to share their partner's story. Elbows on knees to steady himself, one camper took a deep breath and recounted what he'd heard from his walking companion, a young woman who had seemed skeptical and guarded the night before: "What I wish the people I worked with as well as the investors thinking about putting money into my company knew about me is . . . that I have a rare blood cancer and, if my treatment over the next six months doesn't succeed, I'll be dead within the year."

We gasped.

Revealing her secret, something only her husband and a few close friends knew, spoken aloud, broke open her warrior heart. She'd kept the secret to protect the people with whom she worked. She'd kept the secret for fear that the investors wouldn't fund a dying woman's company. She carried the burden of that secret so that everyone who had believed in her, who had given up so much to help realize the dream of her company, wouldn't be at risk if the company couldn't secure the next round of financing.

In that circle, she began to feel the shift that comes from taking your seat as the authentic, true, frightened, deeply feeling adult that you are.

Weeping, she interjected, "And I thought this was going to be just another boring leadership workshop." We burst out laughing, joy added to the grief and fear.

When we stand still, we run the risk of remembering who we are. When we stop the spinning, we run the risk of confronting the fears, the demons who have chased us all our lives. When we stop the bullshitting, the pretending that we're crushing it, that we've got it all figured out, we run the risk of being overwhelmed by the realities of all that we carry—the burdens we're convinced must remain secret to keep us and those we love safe, warm, and happy.

But the spinning prevents us from being who we really are. And perversely prevents the people whom we love, the people we're trying to protect, from knowing, trusting, and seeing us. I know the wish to be seen. I know the need to show up to be seen.

My son Michael and I love movies; it's one of our things. One night, years ago, we went to the movies. He was excited for me to see this film; he'd read the book and was excited to share the story with me.

As the film unfolded, I saw it as a coming-of-age story of a young man, about Michael's age. I even enjoyed the elements that were predictable. Settling in, I watched the film and enjoyed my thoughts about how the main character was (and was not) like Michael. Then, a few minutes before the end of the film, the plot twisted. And suddenly the film was no longer about a boy like my son but more about a boy like I was. It wasn't Michael's life on the screen but mine.

I lost my breath and panicked. I was thrown back in time to my childhood, to events I'd tried so hard to banish from my conscious mind. I wept.

As the film ended and the lights came up and the theater staff moved through the rows, picking up discarded buckets of popcorn, I remained frozen in my seat, weeping, Michael by my side.

Unfrozen and finally able to move, I walked outside with my son, and I let us into my car. Closing the door, and in the safety of the darkened car, I wept some more. And then Michael said it, he gave me the line that showed that, despite his young age, he possessed a deep wisdom.

"Dad," he said, "you might as well tell me what's going on, because if you don't, I'm going to make shit up and it's gonna be negative about me."

Dad, he'd challenged me, you might as well remember. You might as well show up, as you are. You might as well tell me who you are, because if you don't, I'm going to invent things, and those things will stand between us, keeping us from being close.

Until that moment, I hadn't realized that this secret was one of the things I'd wished those who loved me knew about me.

Authentic is such a worn-out adjective; it can feel meaningless. I suppose therefore I prefer grammatically challenged phrases such as "broken-open-hearted warriors." The action that creates true authenticity is embedded in that adjectival phrase. But the call *is* to authenticity. The call is to be real; to show up mad, scared, fearless, or joyful—or all the above.

When clients answer the challenge to stand still, stop the spinning, and be with the truth of their existence, they take their seats as warrior CEOs—strong backs and open hearts.

In the months that followed, the camper facing terminal illness shared her story with not only a wider circle of friends but also her colleagues and, eventually, her investors. Her community rallied and held her—standing still, if you will, alongside her.

The most important part of the story was that the treatment she received worked. She's alive today. But another development shouldn't be overlooked: In sharing her secret, she created the conditions in which her colleagues could share her burden. She was no longer the self-appointed guardian of their safety; they came together to care for each other.

I see it all the time. When leaders, parents, lovers choose to share the reality of their heart, it gives everyone in their lives the chance to know them, to hold them—to trust each other.

I'm reminded of another client. He came to me worried because, after weeks and weeks of assuring his employees that their financing was a sure thing and that a term sheet for a new round of capital was "just days away," he had to face the reality that the investors had broken their word and were backing away.

"What do I tell them?" he asked me, quaking in fear.

"How about the truth?" I suggested.

"The truth? Are you kidding me? If they find out that investors are bailing, they'll hit the streets. Résumés will be flying out the door."

"Well, would you rather they stay for a lie?"

He told the truth and they stayed. Not only did they stay,

but they volunteered to take pay cuts to help the company manage its cash.

"Honey." Once again, I hear Pema Chödrön's voice. "Honey, whatever it is, you're not opening to it. You think you're open. But you're not. You need to keep opening."

We don't stand still because we are afraid of what we will find. We don't share what's really going on because we have misguided notions of dutiful caretaking. These warped, childlike views serve only to exacerbate our isolation and, contrary to what we've been taught, destroy trust. I often think of the moment after we've chosen to stand still as one in which we're faced with a threshold, a doorway.

There are, of course, risks if we share too much. Sometimes, in the guise of radical self-inquiry, we tip over into what some may call radical transparency. Too often, though, we convince ourselves that we are being transparent when what we're really doing is shifting the responsibility onto others. "Here," we wordlessly say, "I can't bear my anxiety, so you carry it for a while."

But I think the far greater risk of standing still, opening to what *is*, is that we may end up remembering our name.

LIFE AT THE TOP OF THE PYRAMID

Shame keeps us from remembering. Shame and fear of being humiliated that our inner doubts will be revealed and the persistent whispery voices calling us unbearable names will turn out to have been right all along.

But an equally dangerous conceit keeps us from taking our seats as broken-open warriors. That is, an insidious need to see ourselves as the only one capable to lead. So, there we sit, alone in our struggles, burdened by the weariness of all the intellectual and externally generated demands, decrying the inability of anyone else in the organization, the family, the state, or—dare I name it—the relationship, to make a *damn* decision.

When working with a group, I'll often jump to a whiteboard and draw a simple triangle. "What is this?" I'll ask again and again until we zero in on their internalized views of hierarchy. "And who sits atop this pyramid?" The boss—"el Jefe"—me, the president, our parents, or even God?

In dissecting this internalized view, we reveal how we buy into the trap of the pyramid of a classic command-and-control organizational structure out of an attempt to quiet the whispery voices of our perceived inadequacies. But it doesn't work. The whispery voices in your head know better. They know that, sitting atop the pyramid, pretending to always have it together, always knowing the answers, is a delusion. Moreover, the delusion is a double bind.

On the one hand, those voices know that, often, we haven't a clue as to how to proceed. In that knowledge, we live with the fear of being unmasked as an impostor. But, on the other hand, the shame of our not knowing leads us to believe that everyone else *does* know; everyone else has it all figured out. Then we do something particularly clever: we turn our shameful fear into further evidence of our failings as leaders, as adults, as humans. So, we spin, we bullshit, and play along in the shell game in which the bean of truth keeps disappearing under swiftly shifting shells.

We sit atop the pyramid, pretending we know. Our colleagues outwardly bemoan our inability to delegate and share authority and inwardly revel in the relief that that they don't have to bear the consequences of a poor decision. And everyone plays the shell game.

The game goes on and on. Slowly then, organizations become a fertile field where we plant the seeds of our childhood struggles. Slowly, inexorably, the top-down inauthentically led group becomes a canvas where we paint out scenes of our past. Slowly, assuredly, team members then respond in kind, replaying the struggles of their families of origin.

Another of Carl Jung's admonitions reverberates: "Until you make the unconscious conscious, it will direct your life and you will call it fate." We look at our organizations and logically conclude that they are fated to be dysfunctional messes. That we, because of our lack of skill, are fated to fail as leaders. To never feel safe enough, warm enough, or happy enough.

There's the Dad, pretending that all is well even as his tense body can only relax with a Pabst Blue Ribbon in hand. There's the Mom, talking to Christ not in prayer but as if he'd pulled up a chair and were sharing a pack of Winstons. And there we are, playing the same games of hide-and-seek, half in and half out, there but not there. And there we all are, collectively pretending that the product works, the company's future is bright, and that we all love and trust each other.

It was January. I'd flown back to New York from my home

in Boulder for a week of client work. The skies were sharp and clear, blue and crisp as the skies of Colorado, and the heavy gray clouds that normally dominate New York winters were nowhere to be seen.

I met the senior leaders of my client's company in a windowless conference room. The group, all twenty-five of us, shared the tasks of arranging the chairs into a circle, the better to be real with one another. No desks or conference tables to hide behind. No walls of intellectualized rigmarole to keep us from seeing what was really going on.

As I often will in group settings, I opened the session reading from Lao Tzu's ancient poem: "Always we hope / someone else has the answer, some other place will be / better, / some other time, / it will turn out/ . . . This is it."

There is no point in peering out a window, he admonishes, or looking to someone for the answer. The answer, I told them, is right here, in the middle of the room.

So, what was the question we'd gathered to sort through? Why was the company so damned conflict avoidant?

My client was one of the co-founders, and the company itself was incredibly successful. In its brief history, its gross revenues had grown to more than $1 billion and its business model was being replicated in other categories across the landscape. It was striving to blend doing well by doing good.

As a result, the company was, in a word, beloved. But its patina of nice belied a deeper truth. Not only were most of the leaders conflict avoidant but, like the boot-camper with his greedy head of sales, they'd outsourced their unacceptable feelings, their naturally occurring aggressions, and projected them onto two members of the senior team who constantly battled each other and belittled each other's teams.

Moreover, these two each reported to one of the two co-founders, personifying and amplifying the split and unresolved conflicts between the leaders. Overtly nice and covertly devious, the management team led lives of quiet, seething anger. Quietly avoiding any hint of conflict. So nice.

Pacing the room, I probed. Turning to one of the co-founders, I asked, guessing really, "Did you grow up with a lot of violence at home?"

"Violence?" he asked, confirming my word choice. "No. No violence."

Confused and unsure, I turned away. And with my back to him he said, "But we did have a lot of yelling."

Stopped in my tracks, I looked around the room and guessed again: "How many of you grew up in homes with a lot of yelling?" Twenty-three of the twenty-five employees raised their hands.

The problem wasn't conflict avoidance, I pointed out. The problem was fear: leftover childhood fears. Fear of the consequences of anger. And because the most senior people had never acknowledged the ways their leadership styles, the choices they made as leaders, were rooted in old patterns, the patterns were replicated and amplified.

The problem, I added, wasn't the two cultural misfits who couldn't get along with each other or the rest of the team. The problem was that they'd all collectively bought into the game of hiding the truth.

Until the leaders embrace the entirety of their pasts, until they acknowledge the collective wish to sweep all conflict under the rug, the conflicts will be driven underground. That doesn't mean they'll stay buried. Instead, they reemerge, with others voicing these roles, proxies for others' resentments and frustrations.

It takes a warrior's courage to stand still long enough for us to inquire within and remember our past.

THIS BEING SO, SO WHAT?

When I was ten, my father came home one night, just around Christmas, and announced that the company he'd worked for for thirty years or so was closing, and he'd be out of a job. Watching my father struggle over the next few years, bouncing from one union-provided job to another, made me feel that I could never depend on anyone else to employ him. Watching my father lose what little self-confidence he had, I swore I'd never let that happen to me. That view—that I'd always be responsible for my own employment—defined my career choices. As with so many superpowers, the view contained both a dark and light side.

The light side gave me a profound and treasured sense of self-reliance. Come hell or high water, I could always make money. And even if I didn't know how to do something, I could learn. And with enough knowledge, I could do or fix anything.

The dark side of that self-reliant superpower has shown up as an antsy unease. Making it difficult for me to stay put for too long. But even that dark side has its own light side. The unease has led me through multiple lives.

Dozens of events shape our careers, our lives. There are the little conversations at the end of the day, over a cup of coffee, that reframe everything. There are the daily mantras we grow up with that shape our values and our sense of the right thing to do in life. And there are the large events, like when my father lost his job, that cause us to take on a new point of view—a demon, if you will. In my case, that view has sometimes cost me but often caused me to push ahead, to try different things, to explore, to take risks. In a way, I wouldn't be the man I am today had I not watched my father struggle through his years of un- and underemployment and had it not been capped by that fearful advice he'd given me about the monkey's ass showing. For good or for ill, and in full-blown rebellion against my father, I've never been afraid to let more of my ass show.

Today, as a coach, I consider myself one of the luckiest people alive. I get to help people by listening deeply and holding on to their stories while they do their work. And among all the things I find so remarkable are the ways in which our lives are shaped by these conversations from our pasts.

It helps to understand the stories of our lives. It helps to see clearly the ways in which a word or two changes everything. Seeing the patterns that ripple out from those tossed stones of events, conversations, and interactions allows us—if nothing else—to remember even more clearly how we became who we are. As I often say with my clients, a good first step to figuring out where you want to go is remembering how you got here.

The call to lead well is a call to be brave and to say true things. To say to our colleagues, we're scared, but we still believe. To say that we may be dying—either figuratively because the investors don't believe or, in some cases literally.

If we're truly to inquire within, if we're truly to care to look and remember what it is we believe, if we're to build organizations in which we tell people what's really going on lest they "make shit up," then we must be willing to open to the reality of life just as it is. Several years ago, I bastardized an old Zen saying I'd stumbled upon. I've repeated my version so often that I can't recall the original. But my version feels more resonant perhaps because of my own lifetime of hiding: *This being so, so what?*

Time and again I've watched hearts break open, so that true and authentic leaders can emerge. But that process depends on a brave first step: facing the reality of what is and not being deluded by the powerful, seductive dreams of what can be.

Of course, this doesn't mean there's no role for dreams. We need dreams. But willfully ignoring what is true is not the same as dreaming. It's delusion; and delusion leads to terrible decisions and, even worse, the destruction of trust.

The first act of becoming a leader is to recognize this being so. From that place, we get to recognize what skills we need to develop and who we really are (and are not) as leaders, and to share our truth in a way that creates authentic, powerful relationships—with our peers, colleagues, and families. Grant us leaders who can do this and we just may create institutions that are less violent to the self, our communities, and our planet.

To open to the reality of life as it is—this is the greatest challenge of all.

Or, put more clearly, the call is to stand still and do the work of self-inquiry. Remember who you are, what you believe about the world, and then, risks be damned, lead from that place of broken-open-hearted warriorship.

Journaling Invitations

Who is the person I've been all my life?

———

What can that person teach me about
becoming the leader I want to be?

———

What was the story my family told about being
real, being vulnerable, being true?

———

What do I believe about vulnerability
and how might that serve me?

CHAPTER 5

———

The Immense Sky of
the Irrational Other

We sat at the kitchen table, a lit Winston burned in the Bakelite ashtray. My dad, in his usual seat at the head of the table, and I, to his right, picking at a tear in the vinyl tablecloth. My mom, in an apron, paced around the kitchen, walking in and through the swirling cigarette smoke.

"I met Art Garfunkel in the bowling alley on Snyder Avenue." My mom talked but it wasn't clear whom she was speaking to.

I looked up from my bowl of Cap'n Crunch, the spoon dripping milk, and braced myself. "Shit," I said to myself, "she's starting up again, Where the hell is this gonna go?" I tried to catch my father's eyes, but he stared at his opened copy of the *Daily News,* his Parker pen in hand fixing the paper's typos.

"Your father was bowling with his league and I was waiting for him to finish up. I had bowled a 154 about an hour earlier so I was pretty happy. The 154 was my new league high . . ."

My body tensed; I watched Dad's reactions. Nothing but the scratch-scratch of his pen on the paper.

"Anyway, I was sitting there, waiting for your father, when this tall, skinny kid with a big mop of hair sits on the stool next to me. He was about your brother's age, eighteen or nineteen, and he was too skinny. All the kids were skinny then because they were all on drugs. You know that drugs do that, don't you?"

She looked at me for permission to continue. I nodded.

"Okay, so I'm waiting for your father and this skinny kid with a blond mop of hair walks in to the alley and takes the stool at the snack bar right next to me. 'Just a burger, please,' says the kid. 'A burger and a glass of water.' So, I asked him, 'Don't you want no fries or nothing?'

"Well, he turned and looked at me like I was some kind of a ghost or something. 'No,' he says. Real slow and spooky-like. 'Are you all right?' I say to him. Well, at that he perked up and we got to talking. He told me his name. Garfunkel, he says, Art Garfunkel. It was a pretty funny name, so I never forgot it. Later, when I heard it all over the place I knew him."

I nodded.

"Anyway . . . .That's why he wrote that song, because of me. You know, 'Mrs. Robinson.' That's me. I'm Mrs. Robinson."

"Fuck! Is it me?" I asked myself silently, "Am I crazy?"

"Dad," I said out loud, trying to disrupt her flow. No response. "Dad!"

"Whaaat?" He looked up from his paper and into my eyes. In the silence, with my eyes, I pleaded with him to do something, to say something. He shrugged.

I finished my cereal, washed my bowl at the sink, and turned to look at her. An apron covered her burnt-orange sweater and polyester slacks. She'd lit her own Winston and taken a drag on a cigarette; the exhaled smoke encircled her head. Slowly, coldly, to reassure myself of the ground beneath my feet and the reality of my world, I turned to my mother: "You are *not* Mrs. Robinson." I stared at her, daring her to say something. She stared back with only a sliver of recognition of who I was.

"Hey, hey, hey . . . ," said my father. "Don't talk to your mother like that."

"Like what? Dad, this is crazy."

"Your mother is not . . . she's not . . . just don't talk like that. Just don't upset your mother." Don't. Don't. Don't. Upset. Your mother. Don't.

I stood and walked into my room. I wrote a note to my brother John: "I can't take it. Not sure when I'll be back. Not sure if I'll be back."

Koo-koo-ka-choo, motherfucker, koo-koo-ka-choo. Koo-koo-ka-choo; get me the fuck out of here.

I grabbed my jacket and headed out the door. Choking on the words I wanted to shout back, I ran out and away, making my way to the A train, to Brooklyn, to Coney Island.

Being fifteen was hard. I often found myself pushing back

against my father, against my mother, against a world that was confusing, insensible, infuriating, and frightening. It was a time when Mom's crazy, irrational rants frightened me less while Dad's shrugging shoulders and his "Whatareyagonna-dobout it?" ways enraged me more.

"Don't talk like that," he'd say over and over. "You'll upset her. Don't upset your mother." *Whatever you do, don't upset your mother.*

In the shadow of the Wonder Wheel, I hid amid the seagull shit and axle grease at its base where, as I once wrote in a poem, I hid my heart—buried it, if you will—in the sand beneath the boardwalk. I was hiding and, yet again, wishing to be found.

My father's fear-filled admonition was seared into my body like a brand. I distinctly remember one of the few times he and I ever talked about it, about what her crazy rants did to him. He told me of the toll it took on his body but, as with so much about my mother's illness, it was only obliquely referred to, approached from an indirect angle.

Like so many times before, we sat at the kitchen table, another burning Winston in the black ashtray. My father had taken his seat and I mine, pulling at the white cotton threads beneath the torn vinyl tablecloth.

After he'd lost his first job, he was low man on the totem pole, and the best the union could do was get him work at another printing company. Every night, precisely at nine thirty, he'd call home from work to see how we were all doing. "I never knew what to expect," he told me. "I never knew if your mother would be upset or not. Sometimes I was so scared that my gut would clench and I would get the runs."

Like so many of us, I cared for both of my parents. So much so that I inherited my father's gut-clenching fear. "Don't upset your mother," entered my body and came out as "Don't upset the Other." It manifested as an obsessive vigilance wherein I learned to watch the Other's every step, every breath, every pause, or furrow of a brow for clues as to what they might say or do next. The vigilance was honed until it became, if you will, a skill, a superpower, all in service to not upsetting the Other.

In the process of our becoming, the admonitions of our parents, the rules by which our families operated and created a sense of belonging, become the rules upon which our survival depends. "Don't upset your mother" carried not only an implicit warning—it is dangerous to upset your mother—but a guideline for dealing with the world, with other people—with the *Other*, even those we see as crazy: *"Don't upset the Other."*

To belong, to be a member of the tribe, safe from being thrust out of the only home we know, we internalize the task of making sense of the Other. Then, when the Other acts irrationally—or, importantly, with a rationale that we can't discern, we get ensnared in a logical trap: It's dangerous to upset the Other. So, our "job" is not only to keep the Other from becoming upset but to bring the Other back to making sense, to not being upset. We become the guardians of those who should be protecting us. We task ourselves with being the firm ground upon which they can stand despite their unsteadiness.

Cold, scared, confused, and under the Wonder Wheel at the age of fifteen, I began for the first time to see the futility of trying to engage with the Irrational Other. I began to see the trap. I stood up, shouting, "Fuck!" I turned to the sea and declared: "This is *not* going to be my life," and fell to my knees, shaking, sobbing.

Looking back now, I see that moment as a declaration of freedom, an intention to free myself from the patterns of behavior and belief that had been shaped by my family life. When I returned home later that same evening, my father was shocked; he hadn't even noticed I'd been gone.

My brother John met me in my bedroom, "Are you okay?"

"Yeah," I said. We hugged and we cried.

"Don't do that again," he said, laughing and crying. "Don't you leave me," he added. "But if you do, you'd fucking better take me with you."

I watched him walk away and turned to rip a page from my black-and-white marble composition notebook, my journal. I wrote a note: "It's absolutely irrational to try to argue rationally with someone who is being irrational." I pulled a photo from a bent, clear Lucite frame, tossed it aside, and slipped the note inside, leaving it on my dresser top where I would see it every day for the next few years.

To hell with not upsetting your mother. To hell with not upsetting the Irrational Other. I was not going to live that life, under the weight of my father's gut-clenching, runs-inducing fears.

Looking back over the decades that followed, I came to understand that this wasn't merely my work. To be free, each of us must come to understand the causes and conditions of our childhood. For these gave rise to the rules by which we, as adults, live—the rules whose original purpose was to keep us safe and that create the conditions we desperately want to change.

GHOSTS IN THE MACHINE

Software developers, borrowing from writer Arthur Koestler, define left-over, outmoded code, no-longer-useful subroutines, buried deep within a current version of a program as ghosts in the machine. While once useful, this outmoded coding starts to get in the way of current operations.

Like everyone, I have millions of lines of such code, operating instructions for how to navigate the world and relationships, which add up to hundreds of ghosts in the machine of my mind.

When I encounter an irrational person, I still avoid arguing. My first impulse is to stifle my feelings. When that fails, I flee. I physically leave. But if I can't physically remove myself, I disassociate—the true "me" will hide and the meat bag of me will stay put: hidden but not hidden, there but not there.

When those strategies fail, I'll turn to making sense of the insensible and try to comprehend the incomprehensible. My journals are filled with diagrams of arguments, lawyer-like briefs, and lots and lots of enumerated points; as if I've become a trial lawyer, a prosecutor, extracting some odd sense of justice.

Journaling. Constantly journaling. Replaying again and again the scenes of the irrational encounter, refining ex post facto rationales I could have used, should have used. My ghosts shape every aspect, let alone every relationship, of my life but they're most powerful when I encounter the Irrational Other.

THE IRRATIONAL OTHER

What makes the Other irrational? Sometimes it's because they're downright crazy; they are dealing with extreme disorders of the mind. But more often it's simply because the rules they live by, the ghosts in their machines, are simply . . . different.

Even then, it's more than simply the differences that can cause each of us to seem irrational to someone else. Usually, the lack of awareness, the lack of understanding of why we do what we do—coupled with our inability or unwillingness to explain the roots of our rules—convey the sense of irrationality.

A co-founder may look at my extreme vigilance, for example, and see only a replication of my father's obsessive focus on correcting others' mistakes, their typos. Without my own radical self-inquiry and, further, my willingness to explore that tendency in the safety of an adult relationship, they're left without the understanding that that passive-aggressive "correcting" is rooted in the effort to stay safe.

Moreover, without my own exploration of the roots of that, I stand little chance of changing behavior others find irrational and frustrating. In my attempt to feel safe and that I belong, I may inadvertently drive away the very people who could best help me feel loved, safe, and that I belong.

These ghosts in the machine maintain themselves; the coding replicates and mutates, embedding deeper and deeper in the relationships that define our loves and our lives.

Encoded in the operating systems of our minds, such ghosts unconsciously determine who gets chosen as our partners and precisely the ways they drive us nuts. Moreover, the places we work, our professional lives, can also become a suffocating web of complex reenactments, the tripwires of past traumas laid out where unsuspecting colleagues are bound to trigger us.

Dealing with what I've come to see as this never-ending supply of Irrational Others is the number one challenge facing many of the entrepreneurs with whom I work.

"I just can't deal with him," she says. I sense her pacing the floor as she speaks to me on the phone. "He says he'll do something and then he up and leaves. He'll leave early on a Friday. Or, worse, tell me that he's headed out for vacation and then delay his return, despite assuring us all that he'll be back in time for the work." Her breaths came faster and faster as she shared her frustration, "and when he does, finally, return, he says nothing about his broken promises."

She's CEO and the "he" is her co-founder. They've been together for years. I've been working with the CEO for just over a year and in that time occasionally had sessions—walks and deep talks—with her co-founder. Despite the company's success, it still felt stuck, mired in a swamp of indecision, infighting, and toxic back-biting.

To the folks who interviewed for jobs at the company, the place seemed idyllic. The beautiful offices hummed with a lively and genuine care for their work in the world. But after months of working together, and developing trust with my client's colleagues, I sensed their feelings, too, of a subterra-nean *wrongness* pervading the office.

The wrongness in the office presaged the wrongness, the "something is off," in the relationship between my client and her co-founder. But, like the office, by all outward appear-ances, the relationship was idyllic. Yet, in private, each thought the other was at fault.

Sorting it out was more than just a matter of sorting through the she said/he said; more than a matter of picking a side and saying who was "right." I'd stepped into a deeply codepen-dent relationship akin to the most dysfunctional marriages I've known, where each side of the pair called the other "stub-born," "closed-minded," and "irrational."

Her impulse, like the impulse of nearly all my clients, was to analyze the Irrational Other to figure out what was wrong with them so that they could be fixed, changed, made better. That was often a cover for another impulse, which was to figure out what was wrong with the Other so that they could justify the ending of the partnership, overcoming guilty feelings.

Thinking back to my boot-camper and his greedy head of sales, I asked the CEO a similar question: "Okay, if he's so awful, why after all these years haven't you fired him?"

We began to unpack the relationship. How did it begin? "He was a visionary," she shared. "I needed him so much."

She told stories of late-night gripe sessions and even later-into-the-night sessions of plotting their escape from the Euro-pean Global 100 company where they'd worked. In the earliest days, there was a third, a mutual friend who was the technical genius. The three of them had made a great team.

"What happened to the friend?" I asked.

"Oh, we kicked him out after the first year—he wasn't pulling his weight."

Three becoming two made me curious. What was at play here? What was really going on in this relationship? To be clear, the company's work had been amazing. They'd built an incredibly successful company. They were making a difference in the lives of millions of people. Still, the undercurrents of dissatisfaction and resentment were as much a part of the culture as their expressed desire to create something lasting and beautiful.

A breakthrough came when my client described how uncomfortable—her word—she was when her co-founder had approached her with some genuine and authentic concerns. Earlier in the week I'd encouraged him to speak directly with her. In doing so, he'd triggered a level of contempt in my client she had not realized she'd felt for him.

"Worse than promising something and failing to deliver was having him cry and tell me he was scared," she said, nearly yelling and clearly angry with me. "I think I need him to be disappointing and emotionally distant."

I reflected back to her what she'd just said: "You need him to be a disappointing and emotionally distant man."

"Oh, fuck," she said, seeing a connection, a ghost in her machine, "He's my father." Her father was a man whose ability to be emotionally present depended on alcohol, whose drinking often ended in long, unexpected disappearances, and whose returns were marked by a terrifying secretiveness, since neither of her parents ever spoke about the fact that Dad had disappeared.

It was and is much more complex than that, of course. But

that was and is one deep and unconscious component of their decadelong codependency: She needed to have a partner who, in effect, promised her freedom ("He was a visionary"; "We plotted our escape together"; "He wouldn't mention his broken promises") but disappointed her time and again, with the greatest disappointment being the untrustworthy illusion of emotional intimacy.

On his side, he needed to disappoint the in-charge, take-charge woman who saw in him a promising future. He was unconsciously compelled to repeat his childhood scenes of having a mother whose wishes for her son would be dashed time and again.

They'd tried for years to break the dynamic. They'd hired consultants to redo their tiny organizational structure, thinking the root of the problem was that they were not dividing the work between them well enough.

All the time, neither suspected that the feeling of being stressed by too much work and not enough time was, in fact, hardwired into their relationship. As part of the complex, family-of-origin-based coding, they each needed to blame the other for the continuous sense of not having enough time. "If only *they* worked harder/smarter/longer, then I wouldn't be so stressed."

Once we laid bare the roots of the antipathy between these two people, who loved each other, we began to see the ways other encoded messages dictated the cadence and rhythms of their lives. The ways, for example, they unconsciously excluded any third person from becoming a senior member of their team, thus inhibiting the growth of the business. Ten years after founding, the senior team consisted of, well, the two of them.

Or the ways in which they would each—confidentially, of

course—share a perspective on the real goings-on at the business. Or the ways that, despite their constantly complaining about the other, neither one was taking ownership of his or her part in the mess of their relationship. The fingers always pointed at the other; the inquiry never went inward.

All those ghosts in the machine, forgotten but still operating subroutines—outliving their usefulness and limiting our growth.

I think of the pair of venture capitalists who tied their fates to each other. One, my client, was by all appearances kind, caring, thoughtful, and beloved. His founding partner? Irrational, hated by the communities of entrepreneurs and co-investors with whom their firm did business. I fielded questions from throughout the start-up ecosystem: "Why would he [my client] pick *that* guy as his partner? That guy's a jerk."

Few—including my client until we unpacked it—understood that the jerk provided a much-needed bad guy for my good-guy client to hang out with. Always the good guy who did what was expected, my client needed to have an evil doppelgänger with whom he could do drugs and party all night.

"If he drives you crazy; if he risks the firm, your reputation, and everything that you've built," I asked him one day, "why do you keep him on?"

He laughed.

Through the laughter, he said, "I have no fucking idea." And he laughed some more.

I pointed out the laughter and asked, "How old do you feel?"

Startled, he said, "I don't know but I feel like I'm in middle school, getting away with pranks and hoping not to be caught."

From that brief recollection of a feeling, we unpacked the

ways he was a good Catholic boy, an altar boy, a choir boy, and that what he really wanted to be was a cool kid. His badass partner made him feel like he was finally a member of the cool kids' club, even as the adult in him recognized the danger.

When the Irrational Other is a sibling or a romantic partner, the complexities quickly multiply.

I think of three different pairs of siblings, co-founders whose decades-old struggles were rooted in late-night, shared-bedroom arguments over whom Mom and Dad loved more. Think of the sibling rivalries no longer playing out over Hot Wheels and the "unfairness" of chores but over product direction and whether the company should take money from a particular investor.

Stepping into a first meeting with one particularly troublesome pair of siblings, I had to shout to be heard over their argument. Thrust into the role of a refereeing parent, I remember laughing as I reprimanded them: "Stop it. Stop this fighting or I'm walking out and never coming back."

And one brother, a thirty-year-old man, looking up with sheepish eyes and a hangdog face, saying, "But he started it."

"Yeah?" asked the other. "Well, you've been doing that to me my whole life." They said this in the boardroom of their four-hundred-person company.

Or when one sibling takes the seat as the CEO and the other as the head of product. The lines of authority should be clear, but they aren't because the product-head sibling is also a board member and he is, technically, his sibling's boss.

The challenges for business partners who are also life partners have a unique expression of this conscious/unconscious dance. One or both partners may feel both manifestations of the partnership (life and business) affected by ghosts from the family of origin, past romantic relationships, and/or past work experiences.

One client, a woman I'll call Virginia, was the founder and CEO of her company. Growing up admiring a thoughtful, successful but emotionally distant entrepreneurial father, she tried to emulate her father's style. Shortly after founding the business, the CEO began dating her chief technical officer. A little later they married. The tensions around emulating her father—including his emotional distance—led all her employees, including her CTO/husband, to never know where they stood and thus to assume that nothing they did was ever good enough for Virginia.

Despite the insistence of the irrationality, the wrongness of the Other, we are never truly alone in our relationships. We are always accompanied by our ghosts.

As in so many relationships, this complex interweaving of self and Irrational Other relies on a combination of psychological transference. The Irrational Other becomes a stand-in for someone in our lives, usually from our past. They become a screen onto which we project our negative and positive qualities, those we can't allow ourselves to acknowledge as our own.

One partner's understandable impatience and focus on effectiveness strike us as "irrational" because it reminds us of the ways we constantly disappointed a parent. That "irrational" behavior then triggers our shame, causing us to withdraw, hide, or make a process overcomplicated, increasing the Other's sense of impatience.

But the merry-go-round of transference and projection doesn't stop there. Often, our unconscious will work to preserve the disappointment/shameful hiding/more disappointment structure because, buried deep within us is the belief that however miserable the complex may make us, at the very least it tells us we're alive.

To the child who lives within us and according to the ghosts in the machine, these complex duets feel like home. The drama and the misery tell us we're safe. We know this pattern because we've been tracing it all our lives.

When I can sense a complex structure such as this is at work behind the incessant complaining about the Irrational Other, my work shifts to helping the parties see the ways the complex structures may have outlived their usefulness. "Put down the script," I'll tell them. "You don't have to be an actor in that drama anymore."

THE IMMENSE SKY

"I don't want to play anymore." I'm whining, and I can't help it. "I want to hand back the script and stop playing the role." This time I'm speaking with Sharon Salzberg. Years after her book *Faith* broke open my heart, she'd become my teacher and someone I sat with in meditation on a regular basis. Someone who could help me sort through the ghosts in my machine, ghosts who would make decidedly unforgettable appearances following meditation sessions.

We're discussing yet another agonizingly perplexing relationship in which I'm twisted, trying to make sense of my fears that the Irrational Other will explode in anger. "Don't upset your mother" bounces in my head.

"All beings own their own karma," Sharon reminds me, referring to the Buddhist law of cause and effect, "their happiness or unhappiness depends on their actions, not my wishes for them." All beings, I realize, including my mother, including the Irrational Other.

With *lovingkindness* for myself (a powerful lesson from Sharon) I allow all the feelings of the irrational, perplexing, agonizing relationship to wash over me. Suddenly I see it clearly: my whining, my sense that I'm trapped by this relationship, my seeming powerlessness over the irrationality of the Other are reenactments. And with that observation I'm suddenly freed from the burden, the trap of trying to make the irrational rational. Not only is it completely irrational to argue with the Irrational Other, it's irrational to try to alter them so that they make sense to me.

In that moment, I realized that we all have a choice in the experience of the Other. We can remain stuck. Or we can allow the Irrational Other to provoke us, to wake us up to the repetition of painful habits and—with love and understanding for ourselves and an embrace of the ghosts in the machine—we can move past any fear or shame and take a step on the path of awakening. We ask: How, indeed, have I been complicit in creating the conditions I say I don't want? More to the point, what am I willing to give up to stop being complicit?

The poet Rilke warned that to love another is "perhaps the most difficult of all our tasks." He also said that implicit in being in a relationship with the Other is "the possibility of always seeing each other as a whole and before an immense sky." But doing so demands realizing and accepting that even between the closest people, infinite distances exist.

Within those distances, beneath that immense sky, lies the possibility of our deepest, most radical self-inquiry: "How am I complicit in creating the conditions I say I don't want?"

The key to understanding is seeing clearly your own re-action. When you react with anger, fear, greed (or even with laughter, as in the case of my client and his wish to be bad), it gives you a chance to see yourself more clearly.

Radical self-inquiry is the path to seeing habits and patterns. Questions that drive us toward that insight are endlessly helpful:

- "What parts of me are being projected onto the other person?"

- "How do I reclaim those parts of me?"

- "What do my reactions say about me?"

- "Why do I do what I do?"

- "Why do they do what they do?"

- "What need for love, safety, or belonging might they be trying to meet with their *irrational* behavior?"

Awakening is damn hard. When our wires are tripped, and the ghosts of the past screech, "It's happening again!" it's damn hard to stand down, to stand still, and inquire within.

How can we disregard our fiery demand that the Other apologize, stop their nonsense at once, and change forever?

If in response to the failing, disappointing, Irrational Other, we are able to inquire deeply and name what it is we're seeing, what's really happening for us, we're often able to break the spell cast by our ghosts.

"HOW AM I COMPLICIT IN CREATING THE CONDITIONS I SAY I DON'T WANT?"

Ann was struggling mightily. Her co-founder, Paul, was, in her words, "incredibly indecisive" and "buffoonish and slow." Even though she was the CEO, he, as the head of strategy for the company, used his position as a board member to "lord it over her," she said, and "disrespect her by telling her what to do."

Ann and Paul's friendship went back to college, and when they finished up graduate school, both Harvard Business School alums, they decided to launch a business together. They'd sat up late, night after night, with white sheets of paper, sketching out ideas. "Ann's a natural executer," Paul told me the first time we met. "I'm all about the big ideas but Ann really gets shit done." It made sense that she should take on the responsibility of being CEO, he added, because he knew she was simply better at making the quick decisions. But lately she'd been making too many decisions without consulting him, and not only had he felt steamrollered but the once-critical balancing act between their decision-making styles no longer worked. He felt diminished and disrespected. Their differences seemed irreconcilable.

Having worked with each of them, I know each of them was speaking a truth—at the very least, their feelings were true, even if, objectively, the facts were slightly different from the perspectives they held. I encouraged them to use the practice of mindfulness as a form of radical self-inquiry to break the spell gripping each of them and to alter the course of their interactions.

Unbeknownst to each of them, I had given them the exact same instructions when they'd e-mailed me about how irrational the other was being. Using a particularly incendiary e-mail exchange, with its ever-escalating anger, I encouraged them to put down their weapons, to put down their phones.

"When the 'ding' notifies you of a new e-mail," I wrote to each of them. "Don't answer it. Don't even look at your phone."

I told them to sit, taking note of every feeling that came up, especially the bodily sensation. Note the desire to read the e-mail and note without jumping in, giving in, the stories you might tell yourself about what the e-mail contained. When you find yourself following the story, ask yourself a question about your body. "Where in my body does this story live?"

The point was to encourage them to widen the gap between the stimulus, the "ding," and the response, "I can't believe how wrong he/she is. She/he never respects me."

"It was so painful," Ann told me afterward. "I felt heat rising from my chest and going to the top of my head. I was like one of those cartoon characters where you see the head turning into a teakettle and steam coming out the ears." She laughed as she recognized the deep Pavlovian call to up the ante and once again explain how wrong Paul, the Irrational Other, was.

Instead of steam, Paul reported crying. "I was so overcome by this deep, deep well of sadness. It filled my entire chest cavity."

"How old is that sadness?" I asked him.

"Very old," he said between sobs. "It's me, being slapped one more time by my mother. Me being told once more that I'm just not good enough."

Later, in a joint session, I asked each of them to lean into their awful, spiky pain; those ancient tender spots. "Stay with the bodily sensations," I told them. "Notice but don't board the train of the thoughts that pulls into the station.

"See the stories you're telling yourself about the other," I continued. "What do those stories reveal about the stories that you might have been holding quietly, silently, for all your lives?" We sat in painful silence as they both looked down and straight ahead. After what seemed like an eternity, Ann spoke first: "That I'm cold, uncaring, and focused only on the next step ahead, never on the people I say I love."

"Who told you that story, Ann?" I asked.

"My ex-husband. He said this was why he could not stay married to me."

We honored the weight of that revelation with more silence. We gently turned to Paul.

"I've not lived up to my potential," he stammered. "And never will."

Nodding, leaning forward, my elbows on my knees: "How old were you, Paul, when that story first landed in your body?"

"I was so fucking little. I can't even recall not feeling this way."

Suddenly the air flowed again in the room. All three of us were breathing. Speaking to the two of them, I asked, "Did you know that this is what your friend believes about themselves?"

They looked at each other and I saw two old college friends, no longer the CEO and her co-founder. They saw again the two crazy-assed entrepreneurs who had the audacity to try and change the world. They saw the Other, no longer irrational.

For this is one of the opportunities that the Irrational Other presents: to stand beneath the immense sky and see the Other as whole yet disturbed by his or her own ghosts. Growing up, this Other could never feel safe. The family system ensured that they could never ever relax. Their blend of hypervigilance was designed to do the same thing as mine: keep them safe.

Slowing down or, better yet, standing still and paying mindful attention to oneself, allows one to see past the projections, the stories we tell ourselves about the Other, asking once more, "How am I complicit in creating the conditions I say I don't want?"

The most painful gift of the Irrational Other, then, is the opportunity to see ourselves better. Their irrationality stems partly from our having projected onto them the good and the bad traits that are really ours to claim. Seeing their irrationality in this way is like encountering our reflection in a Coney Island funhouse mirror: It's us, we see, but distorted into a funny, scary imago of us—true but not accurate and frighteningly distorted.

If, as Jean-Paul Sartre observed, hell really is other people, then the truest hell is seeing ourselves in that irrational, distorting mirror.

Relief can come, though, when we gaze at this distortion as if seeing the immense sky containing all our positive and negative traits, as well as those of the Other. What is it about your co-founder's failures as an entrepreneur that disgust and enrage you? Was it perhaps because she saw in him the fact that not only was he not keeping her safe but that she, like him, was failing?

Ann heard something Paul never intended to communicate through his actions. Paul saw in Ann's responses the distorted reflection, his own worst feelings about himself.

If we gaze at that distortion with the mindful curiosity implicit in the self-inquiry process, we can breathe in the reality that each of us is whole, disturbed merely by fragments of leftover code—ghosts. From beneath such a sky, we begin leaning into other radical self-inquiry questions. We get to choose actively our experience of being with the Other, rational or not.

"What are your operating instructions?" I ask the next pair of co-founders who come in with their conflicts. When the ghosts screech at you, when your tripwires are triggered, what do you do? Do you retreat? Do you lash out?

More to the point, how would you like the Other to respond to you? Can you give instructions to dial down your fear and anger? And, for extra credit, when you're responding from your most resourced place—when you feel loved and safe, and your belonging is not threatened—what if you were able to give that feeling to the Irrational Other? What if all he needs is silent understanding and the guardianship of his solitude, so he can work through what his ghosts are demanding he work through?

"Jerry, I'm going crazy," Eliza wrote to me. "Please, can you possibly make time for me?"

A new client, Eliza is the co-founder and CEO of a tiny but fast-growing company. When we first met, the company had twenty employees. Seven months later, they had forty. She had just hired her first chief technology officer and it was about him that she was looking for help.

He was the Irrational Other.

"What'd he do now?" I asked her.

"He always does this. He always leaves without getting his work done and he always leaves without even telling me he's leaving. He's so disrespectful. I think it's because I'm a woman."

Taking a breath, I asked her to tell me more about feeling disrespected. "I know how he feels," she said, trying to stand in his shoes. "He can't stand working for a woman."

"That's true," I said, noting that unconscious bias is even more rampant than overt sexism. "But why would he have taken the job?" I knew she'd just hired him and that he'd accepted the job after turning down higher-paying jobs elsewhere. He had told me, and I was convinced that he was genuine, that he really admired my client and was excited to work for her.

I suggested she use a tactic I learned from training in nonviolent communications: OFNR. O, for observation of undeniable fact. F, for feeling and assumptions about motivation and other interpretations of facts. N, for needs—individual as well as collective needs. R, for request . . . a request for an alternate way of behaving.

"Start with the facts," I told her. He left the office earlier than expected and he did so without telling anyone. "Then," I explained further, "share how his doing so made you feel—in this case, disrespected.

"Then share with him the collective need . . . that everyone in the company has a need to feel respected. Then," I told her, "make a request. If he needs to leave early, ask that he let you know in advance."

"It worked!" she wrote to me a few hours later. It turned out that he'd gotten an emergency call from his wife, their four-year-old daughter had had a raging temperature and needed to be rushed to the hospital. He hadn't said anything about why he was leaving, he shared, because he didn't want to appear weak, like he was putting family ahead of the job.

"Can you believe he thought that putting family ahead of work is something I would think was weak?" she asked.

"Yes, I could," I wrote back. "He's got a ghost in his machine just as you have a ghost that tells you when someone does something unexpected and possibly threatening, it's an existential disrespect."

FORGIVING THE IRRATIONAL OTHER

From Eliza to Virginia to Paul and Ann and the good boy/bad boy doppelgänger investors, each client's experience of the Irrational Other offered the chance to grow. They used the awful, painful experience of being in a relationship to grow up and beyond the confines of their childhoods. In looking in the funhouse mirror the Other presented they saw their ghosts and, in doing so, got to see the fullness of the Other.

Looking backward, I see the brokenness of Mom's childhood as the source of her later "irrationality." It took years of work, but I had finally come to see her ghosts and the way they haunted her. Indeed, when I squint, I can see her father, Dominic Guido, in his fear and bewilderment, feeling so helpless as to, at times, lash out violently. Looking backward, standing side by side beneath the immense sky, I can see her as whole but brokenhearted. Confused, scared, even standing beneath her own Wonder Wheel, trying to make sense of an irrational world.

In seeing her, my archetype of the Irrational Other, as not so irrational but merely human, I get to see myself in exactly the same way.

Late in 2015, after a near-deadly fall, we brought Mom to a nursing facility, where she would die a year later. Shortly after getting her settled into the home, I flew to New York to visit her. Shocked by her frailty, I remember thinking that her hair, which was always so important to her, wasn't right. It was flat, not teased into an *updo*, as it'd normally be. It seemed, if possible, even whiter.

The reality of her eventual death and all that had happened between us seemed frozen in that moment. Here she was, the scary, irrational, crazy Other, the woman who'd time and again left me questioning my own sanity and, sometimes, my desire to live. She was weak, confused, scared in her own right.

Her eyes searched my face as well as the faces of my kids. I see her no longer as the Irrational Other but as the woman who rose each Sunday to make a fresh pot of tomato sauce for our Sunday dinners. In those scared eyes, I see her strength, her ability to overcome the pain and trauma of her life, the unfair and irrational pains she had to suffer. Suddenly, the smell of the antiseptics of a nursing facility are replaced by the mouth-watering fragrance of fresh meatballs stewing in her sauce.

I remember so much. I remember, as the pot bubbles, Dad with a copy of the Sunday edition of the *Daily News*. "Who's got the comics?" he's just asked. "I haven't finished the puzzle yet."

As I stand over her bed, watching her watch my kids, scanning my face, her eyes asking, "What's happening to me?" I remember long, dark walks from our house in Queens to the subway, to the A train. She and I passing Oxford Bakery, with the bakers in the kitchen and the street filled with the smell of apple turnovers and crumb cake. "German bakers," she'd say, "they're the best." In those months after she and I moved in together and before my father and brothers, Dom and John, came to stay with us, together, just she and I would climb the steps to the elevated A train. Every morning at five thirty, so she could get to her receptionist/file clerk job on Wall Street, and where I could make it to school in Brooklyn by eight. We'd sit together on the subway, the heaters below the seats warming our bottoms and calves. Leaning into each other, I'd fall asleep on her shoulder, safe, warm, and filled with the smells from a German baker.

Back in the nursing facility, I am both here, with her, in the months before she has died and, somehow, back there, where the anger and suffering scared me.

However old the trope may be, I feel my father's presence over my shoulder. Though dead for more than twenty-five years, he's with us now. He whispers in my ear something he'd written to me, back when I was in high school. It was the night before the opening of a show. One of the few stage appearances of my life, the year before I'd been picked to play Oberon, the fairy king, in Shakespeare's *A Midsummer's Night's Dream*.

Using his treasured Parker pen, he'd written me a simple note. Even to this day, I can see that looping handwriting: "Good luck," he'd written, "or, as they say, 'Break a leg.'" And then, after a space on the little sheet of yellow paper, he'd added, "No one could be prouder of you than I am right now." I carried that note in my wallet until time and age had disintegrated the paper, its message etched forever into my soul.

Back to Mom, lying there, scared and confused. I thanked Dad for his reminder and I leaned in, speaking directly into her hearing aid–less ear, and said, "It's gonna be all right, Mom. I love you. I forgive you."

"Whaaat?" she said.

Through my tears I laughed. Of course, she couldn't hear it. It didn't matter; I felt it.

Recalling that moment now, thinking about my time in Coney Island as well as all the times I ran away (literally or figuratively), I'm flooded by not only forgiveness but, crazily enough, gratitude. If I had not encountered Mom's irrationality, if I had not actively but unconsciously sought out time and again the ability to reenact being in relationship with the Irrational Other, I would not have discovered my deeper self and all the rich resources that are waiting for me to deploy.

I'm sure I would have been a good person without the rigors of the Irrational Other. I am a good man. But without those struggles, I wouldn't be me. And the truth is, I like being me. So, thank you, Mrs. Robinson.

Journaling Invitations

Why do I struggle with the folks in my life?

———————

Why are relationships so difficult?

———————

What am I not saying to my co-founder, my colleagues, my family members, my life partner that needs to be said?

———————

What's being said to me that I'm not hearing?

———————

CHAPTER 6

Handprints on the Canyon Wall

I *am closer to the age when my father died than I am to the age* *when I first became a father.* That thought, like a whisper on the wind, startled me as I walked around Wonderland Lake, in the foothills of the Rockies. As the midmorning light slanted toward the hills, calling forth their very best pinks and grays; as the overnight dusting of frost sparkled on the flat lake water and crunched beneath my shoes, the thought gnawed at me. As I approach the age when my father passed away, I think of how the repetition of patterns creates a delicate, intriguing symmetry in our lives. I passed from being the young son of a young man to being a young man to being the young father of a boy, then a girl, and then another boy. Each of them, adults now in their own right; my oldest is the same age I was when I became a father and, soon after, said good-bye to Dad.

Reverie interrupted by questions. Step, step, crunch. *Who am I becoming?* Step, step, crunch. *What do I believe to be true about the world?* Step, step, crunch. *As I'm becoming an elder . . . Now what should I do with my life now that I am becoming an elder?* Crunch, cough, cough, sniffle, step.

Sniffles, crunches, and questions were then followed by the words of the poet David Whyte:

> *By the lake in the wood,*
> *in the shadows,*
> *you can*
> *whisper that truth*
> *to the quiet reflection*
> *you see in the water. . . .*
>
> *Remember,*
> *in this place*
> *no one can hear you*
>
> *and out of the silence*
> *you can make a promise*
> *it will kill you to break.*

"[T]hat way," the poet promises, "you'll find what is real and what is not."

What's real? What's not? I'd walked Wonderland with my

colleague Andrew just days before. It was on our third circum-ambulation of the lake when he finally asked the question he'd been carrying: What should I do with my life? Earlier in the week, he'd stopped me at a coffee shop; mid-order, he turned to me: "Can we go for a walk sometime?" His eyes revealed a terror; he expected me to scoff and reject him, to laugh in his face at the absurdity of his idea.

"Of course," I said, "I'd like that. How about Friday, at eleven, at Wonderland?"

Cattails at the lake's edge swayed. The frost glistened as the sun moved toward the center of the sky. He turns to me, "I know this is absurd of me to ask . . . I mean, I'm a coach, too, and I'm supposed to be giving other people advice . . . but, well . . ."

The pause hung. "What?" I asked. "Andrew, whatever story you're telling yourself is likely wrong. Whatever it is that's stopping you from speaking is old, tired, and worn out. Old programming designed to keep you safe. I'm not judging you. I'm just a friend, going for a walk with you."

He burst into tears: "I don't know what to do with my life. I'm forty-four years old and I have no idea if I'm doing the right thing." The tears flowed and his body shook. I grabbed his hands and squared up opposite him.

"Andrew, no one knows if they're doing the right thing. No one. Whatever story you've been telling yourself about how you've failed, whatever 'should' you've been carrying about having had it all figured out by now . . . well, all that's just bullshit, stories told to you by the ghosts in your machine."

Through blurry, teary eyes he looked from our clasped hands

to my eyes, still unsure if I was judging him. "But you've got it all together, you figured out how to make a living doing the thing you love."

I burst out laughing: "Oh, geez. Have I got *you* fooled!"

We started walking again. His questions became pragmatic and structural. "Give me the steps, Jerry. How do I get customers? How do I convince people to hire me? How do I build a business? How do I raise money? How do I hire people? How do I fire people?"

All genuine, important questions but, really, all a proxy for the deeper existential questions: Am I doing it right? Is it supposed to feel this confusing? Will I ever feel safe, warm, and happy? Where do I belong? What do I want from this life? Am I worth it? Have I earned my place on the planet, in this life? And, of course, If my life isn't unfolding as I expected, then what *am* I doing?

"I want to strip everything away," he continued. "Anything that's not me, to the bare essence of me, just so I can figure out what path I should take." I knew that feeling.

Years before, I had knelt before Pema Chödrön, pleading for her to tell me the path, the way, the steps I should take, to take me out of the pain. Then she lovingly tapped my hand, telling me about the pathless path. It makes sense now; then it left me bereft.

"You seem to want to know that you're making progress," I offered. "That there's a path and that you're on it." He nodded with relief.

"It's curious," I continued. "We're all so desperate to move up and to the right. We're convinced that any motion that isn't straight, direct, up and to the right is somehow not part of the path."

What if being lost is part of the path? What if we are supposed to tack across the surface of the lake, sailing into the wind instead of wishing it was only at our backs? What if feeling lost, directionless, and uncertain of the progress is an indicator of growth? What if it means you're exactly where you need to be, on the pathless path?

Opening an e-mail recently, there it is again: the wish for direction, a path: "Dear Jerry," the inquiry begins. "I am looking to define a meaningful next chapter which meets my personal, professional, and practical goals."

And then, opening yet another note: "I'm not lost, but could sure do with a point in the right direction (and a kick up the ass!)."

We all want it: movement that demonstrates that our experience is meaningful; that it's taking us someplace; a place where we are smarter, richer, healthier, less afraid, more secure. *Up, up, and to the right.*

We live in a world that says anything less is failure. Up and to the right, we're told, is where the happy people are. That's where the people who never fear, never fail, never struggle live.

Our economy is driven by the sense that here—down and to the left—is awful and if we buy the right soap, drive the right car, build the right company, love the right way, we'll be safe and loved and happy forever and ever. And ever.

We look to those who seem serene, content—the embodiment of up and to the right—and fail to see the struggles they have lived through. We project onto them our wishes and expectations of reaching that point where all things are at peace and we never, ever have bodily odor. Everyone else's journey is so much easier. Everyone else's business is so much more successful. And if only someone—you—would show me the steps on the path, give me a map, then I can get there, too.

But a map is a poor substitute for a life lived. The truest guide isn't the mind of a guru but your broken, scared and scarred, lonely heart. I just wish broken-open hearts weren't so damned painful.

The irony, of course, is that up and to the right, as appealing as it is when we're down and to the left, is a place of separation. It's a place where, were we to achieve it at all, we'd find ourselves utterly alone.

HANDPRINTS ON THE CANYON WALL

"[T]ucked up in clefts in the cliffs," wrote the poet Gary Snyder in his poem "Anasazi."

Anasazi and their descendants, the Havasupai. I hear their names as I close my eyes and dream of my days visiting the Grand Canyon.

By August 2001, everything was broken. One of the companies I'd invested in, *The Industry Standard* magazine, had been an emblem of the seeming rise and rise of the "new economy." Each weekly issue was fat with ads. Then, suddenly, it all seemed to stop. With the collapse of the financial markets, venture capital stopped flowing to start-ups. With start-ups failing like falling knives, ads dried up. Suddenly caught with too many expenses, management struggled to find a way to right-size our way out of the problem. Infighting, fear, clashes between the investors (myself included) kept us from funding the shortfall. Suddenly we were bankrupt. It was big news, as most of the people who followed the venture-backed technology space also read *The Industry Standard*.

In August 2001, as the news broke, I was hiking down the Kaibab Trail from the North Rim of the Grand Canyon with a group that would spend the next week rafting the Colorado, at the base of the canyon, in the belly of the Earth.

The first stirrings of the unease, discomfort, and pain that—months later—would leave me gasping for air, for life at Ground Zero, had begun just after the market freefall in March 2001. Shortly after, Fred, my partner at Flatiron, and I had begun negotiating with our investors about altering or even shutting down the investment program we'd launched in 1996. I remember tearfully telling Fred that I wasn't sure what was happening to me or what I wanted to do long term, but I knew I couldn't commit to building another investment fund.

I didn't know it, but I was dying inside.

Back in the canyon, I began to both fall apart and sense that there was another way. Three days into the rafting trip, all the stresses of life above the rim had slipped away. I'd lie on my sleeping pad at night, relaxing my gaze to better glimpse shooting stars. I'd discovered that looking for the movement was not the way to see them—an insight that I have come back to time and again in the years since.

The night before we were to visit Deer Creek Canyon—a sacred place where the Havasupai youth would test their adulthood by leaping across a chasm to leave a handprint on the other side—I felt the thinness of my own existence. I realized, as poet David Whyte notes, "how easily the thread is broken / between this world / and the next."

Handprints on the canyon wall, placed as those young warriors entered the temple of their adult aloneness, testified that, regardless of the solitude, they had been there.

I lay in the dark as the dawn broke past the rim, weeping. "What are my handprints?" I yelled at myself. "Some fucking investment? Is this how my passage through and existence in this life is gonna be remembered? Fuck!"

I thought back to the time when, sheltered under the boardwalk at Coney Island I declared: "This is *not* going to be my life!" I wasn't meant to live hidden in the shadows of the boardwalk, weeping.

Suddenly, amid the tears, I had a memory. I remembered walking out of a movie theater with my big sister Mary. She'd taken the seven-year-old me to the Loew's Kings Theatre on Flatbush Avenue, blocks from our home on East 26th Street—between Clarendon Road and Avenue D—to see a Laurel and Hardy film festival. A weird kid, I loved Laurel and Hardy, and Mary loved me and so she wanted me to be happy and took me to see sixty-year-old films. For hours, we'd sat in the darkened Kings.

Afterward, holding hands, swinging arms, we walked to the ice cream parlor; movies and ice cream and swinging arms: love, safety, and belonging.

"What do you want to be when you grow up, Jerry?" she asked. Looking back, I realize she was a kid herself, just in her twenties, and was already the teacher she'd chosen as her profession.

"I don't know," I answered shyly, unsure of what she was really asking me. Pausing before speaking more, I remembered the feeling I often had before falling asleep each night. As I lay in bed, a dark hole in my chest would open up, a hollowness, a loneliness deeper than anything that stemmed merely from being alone.

To close the hole, I'd hug my Howdy Doody doll ever closer. It was a toy; it was supposed to be played with in a particular way. A kid was supposed to use it to put on puppet shows. But not me. I just hugged him, held him, and used him as best as the seven-year-old me could to close that gaping wound, that crack in the bark of my tree.

After becoming a father, I came to realize that not everyone felt that hole in the chest, not everyone saw the hole as evidence of brokenness and unlovability. Still hesitating, I turned to Mary, "I think . . . I think maybe I don't want to be forgotten."

We stopped walking and she turned to see me more clearly, inviting me to say more, "Like, I don't know . . . a hundred years from now, when someone is talking about Flatbush Avenue and the Kings and the people who lived here, I want people to know I was here."

Seen but not seen. There but not there. The boy in the crack of the tree, wishing to leave handprints.

Decades later, I stared at the handprints on the walls of the canyon, deep in the belly of the Grand Canyon. I had fallen apart, just as Pema, in a way, predicted when she had written her book. I looked for my own handprints, evidence that I had passed this way, that I mattered. Then, at the bottom of the canyon, I found a new way to see.

At the end of the rafting trip, we were lifted from the bottom of the canyon by helicopter. Two hours later, I sat at McCarran Airport, stunned by the incessant ding, ding, ding of slot machines, cascading coins, and dreams of a better life. I'd left the canyon, but the canyon never left me.

AFTER GROUND ZERO

Once upon a time, there was a prince who stood not under a boardwalk in Brooklyn but within a castle in northern India, declaring, in his way, that this was not to be his life. He left his father's castle to find himself and ended up under the bodhi tree. Having declared, "Fuck it," he'd given up trying to see the shooting stars and learned to relax his gaze.

We came out of the canyon and into September 11, 2001, and its aftershocks. I had naively thought that market collapses, vanishing wealth, and failing, falling knives of start-up investments were bad. But I hadn't considered the unrelenting terror emanating from Ground Zero. How could I have?

The springtime collapse of 2001, the late-August handprints on canyon walls, the autumnal dying of the light and terrifying rupture of our collective delusions of safety all led inexorably to my collapse. They all led, too, to my transformation and an acceptance of my purpose, my karma, and my reason for being.

It was as if shooting stars, asteroids, and meteors had fallen from the sky, hitting me midway through the journey of my life, and knocking me not merely onto a new trajectory but into the orbit I was born to traverse. Looking backward, I couldn't draw a straight, up-and-to-the-right line defining my path, no matter how hard I tried.

Understanding that this is, in fact, the universal pathless path defies not only the messages of our economy. It defies the daily and relentless propaganda of social media. My friends and family, especially those in their twenties, confound themselves not only by holding themselves to some unrealistic standard of a non-messy, straightforward unfolding of their lives but by comparing their internal mass of contradictions, confusion, and uncertainty with the happy lives they see posted on Instagram.

I say this dramatically, trying to cut through the fog of useless and constant comparison in which we inevitably come up short, less than, and therefore broken and unworthy of love. Dear ones: Newsflash. Snapchat, Instagram, and Facebook lie.

The path to a purpose-grounded life is messy, muddy, rock-strewn, and slippery.

I have a dear friend, a boot-camper, who knew all her life that she liked girls more than she liked boys. But in the Christian household of her childhood, her truest self was quashed because she was believed to be possessed.

I have another dear friend, another boot-camper, who knew her whole life that the gender assigned to her by the world was wrong. Misgendered. Not *her*. She was trapped in a jail made of the bars of others' perceptions. All her life, she played along to *try* to belong, and, playing along, she felt she was slowly dying inside. One night, under the stars of a clear Colorado night, she heard stories of others whose truths were quashed, squashed, and squeezed to fit into someone else's preconception of what it meant to be a CEO, an entrepreneur, a good girl, a good boy, worthy of love, safety, and belonging. She felt their tears. She leaped across the chasm, the false chasm, the one that tells us that the Other's story is not our story and that our story is uniquely bad, or different—further evidence not of our adult aloneness but of our childlike, fearful loneliness. The cause of the deep chasm in the middle of our chest.

In that leap, she touched the handprints of the others who'd leaped their own chasms, and in so doing, she was able to leave her own. Leaving, too, the old identity, unlearning all that had confined her, all that restricted her, all that entrapped her.

She discovered who she is *now*, casting aside the need to know who she will be later. She dared to leave new, truer handprints on the walls of the newest canyon of her life.

The path requires standing still, radically inquiring within, learning to the bear the pain of uncertainty. Discovering your purpose, feeling your way into that aliveness, requires clambering up rocky cliff faces, leaping chasms, tucking oneself deep into clefts and deeper and deeper into the Earth. It demands the willingness to step into the crack of the tree as well as the bravery to step out of it. All this, and good-soled hiking boots.

BUT I NEED A PLAN!

Crunch, crunch, step. My good-soled, low-cut hiking boots slipped and slid as Andrew and I made *kora*, rimming Wonderland.

"But you've got it all together, you figured out how to make a living doing the thing you love . . ." I chuckled quietly, knowing what was coming next. ". . . I need a plan."

"Here's your plan," I said out loud, annoyingly, enigmatically, "stop looking for shooting stars."

I told him about lying on banks of the Colorado River, learning to relax my gaze. "What would it feel like to let go of the need to know?" I asked. He paused and felt what it would feel like in his body, not in his mind, if he let go of not only the need to progress but of the belief in progress.

"What would it feel like, in that body of yours," I continued, "if incremental progress that was directionally correct were enough? What would it feel like to tack across the surface of that lake instead of heading out for the other side, fully intending to make it in the shortest time possible?"

I could sense him turning inward and really considering the feeling. Crunch, crunch. We walked on in silence, and then he broke it: "Relaxed."

I smiled enigmatically and lovingly. "If you could give up the need for measurable progress, if you give up the pursuit of purpose and meaning," I continued, adding, quietly to myself—"and the need to build an exhaustible supply of lemon drops"—"and then focused on doing what is right and true each day, it feels to me that you'd live in congruency with your truest self, where the meaning of your life was a function of the meaning of each day. And each day, an expression of your life."

Early in 2017, I dreamed I was back in Tibet, hiking in a valley outside the city of Yushu. I'd first visited Yushu in September 2010, five months after an earthquake had killed thousands of people and destroyed hundreds of buildings. We'd spent months raising money and we'd brought supplies—winter tents, thick blankets, water—to a community still struggling to recover.

In the dream, I was wearing low-cut hiking boots, clambering among the rocky terrain of a valley, pockmarked with carved images of Tibetan Buddhist saints and the ubiquitous prayer in Tibetan script, Om Mani Padme Hum.

In the dream, I sat down to take a drink when a hole opened in the ground between my bent knees. Peering into the hole, I realized that it was a mine shaft and that it was endlessly deep. Lungta—tiny Tibetan "wind horse" prayer flags, normally tossed at high mountain passes so that the winds can carry the prayers printed on them to the Buddhas of the past, present, and future—fluttered in the shaft.

Peering deep, I saw the Lungta turn into pages of the book of my life.

Scared little boy. Struggling adolescent lost, questioning whether to go to school or even to live. English major, studying poetry with and star-struck by Marie Ponsot. Scholarship winner and, suddenly, struck by a shooting star and set on a new course, a reporter at a technology magazine. Finding myself as my life unfolded, yet still haunted by the sense of being lost.

My twenties became my thirties. My thirties seemed successful: I began collecting lemon drops. Then suddenly struck by another shooting star, weeping in the canyon, falling to my knees at Ground Zero, discovering compassion and the nature of reality through Pema Chödrön's eyes; discovering courage through Parker Palmer's writing; and discovering faith and lovingkindness through the words of Sharon Salzberg.

Still lost, still searching, still struggling to let go of the need for progress that was more than directionally correct, looking for the up-and-to-the-right path, I left my career. Looking for the well-worn, easy-to-travel path, the one where your shoes didn't need to be especially grippy, I crossed the polar ice cap in Greenland, rafted the Futaleufú River in Chile, and, most important, learned to meditate, to stand still even in empty time.

I told Andrew, "My path was anything but straight."

"What if we lived our lives forgetting the destination we're aiming for," I asked. "What if we woke each day and just wondered what will happen today?"

As we continued walking, I was reminded of Joseph Campbell's thought that the pursuit of purpose and meaning is really a pursuit of aliveness, of rapture. Andrew leaned in, his eyes flashed.

"And aliveness, well, I don't know how we are fully alive when we spend all this energy damping down and rejecting the various parts of ourselves."

Dear Professor Campbell, yes, indeed, the pursuit of purpose is really a cover for the pursuit of a feeling, aliveness. But aliveness can come about only after integrating even the most shameful parts of ourselves—even the stories of our misdeeds, mistakes, and missteps. Integrating those and learning to forgive oneself.

"There's something you need to know about me," I told him, "I'm a sucker for Oreos."

In the years before, during, and immediately after my Ground Zero days, I was seventy-five pounds heavier than I am today. Frustrated, angry, disgusted with myself, I hauled my (fat) ass into a nutritionist's office. "Erica gave me a lot of tools," I continued, "including a whole new approach to food." But the most important gift she gave me was the power of "do-overs." I explained that one day I had come to see her, dejected and ready to give up. I whined: 'I ate a fucking dozen Oreos last night, Erica . . . a fucking dozen.'"

"Well, the combination of sugar and salt is deadly for you. Some folks like sweets. Some like salts. You're one of the lucky few," she said with sweet sarcasm, "who craves both. An Oreo is the perfect drug for you." And then she gave me the gift: "Tonight, it's a do-over. Start again."

And suddenly I was twelve and back in Brooklyn, this time on West 7th Street and Avenue T, playing stickball with Paulie, Ugo, and Pino. And we were arguing about whether Paulie's shot was a hit or a foul, and to stop the fighting, Ugo yells "Do-over!" and just like that, all is forgiven, all is forgotten. It's not an out. It's not a foul. It's not a hit. Do-over.

Later—much later—I read Shunryū Suzuki's *Zen Mind, Beginner's Mind* and realized that coming back to the beginner's mind is a do-over. "If I allow myself," I tell Andrew, "then I can have an infinite number of do-overs." I explained that we can always return to what is, what is really happening, what is truly present. Even more powerfully, if we do that, then we can let go of the e-mail, let go of the missed quarter, let go of the shame of having eaten all those Oreos.

ENDLESS DO-OVERS

"If you allow it, each footstep can be a do-over." I was speaking by satellite phone with my client and friend, the polar explorer Ben Saunders, as he was trying to retrace his friend Henry Worsley's path across Antarctica. The sastrugi—the parallel wavelike ridges carved by the polar winds into the surface of icy snow—were tougher than he'd imagined, and he was close to giving up.

The possibility of giving up wears on him. In 2016, his friend, his mentor, Henry, stopped one hundred and twenty-six miles short of his goal of being the first person to cross the Antarctic peninsula unaided and unassisted. Overcome by exhaustion and airlifted out, Henry died in Chile. Ben's trying to complete the journey, to finish his friend's quest. He's been cursing each ridge, he told me; each ridge means he can't really ski but must painfully step up and over.

"Soften your gaze," I told him. Each morning, each step, is a chance for beginner's mind, I continued. I'd recommended Shunryū Suzuki as a companion on this trip, so he understood the reference. "Perhaps you can hold off deciding to continue or not until you make it to the Pole." When the big goal feels too large, take only small steps.

I thought of my advice to Ben as I listened to Hollis, my editor. Midway through the journey of this book, every page, every word felt like a sastruga ridge, with fifty-below headwinds pushing me back. "Just write essays," she counseled. The next week, I reread Anne Lamott's *Bird by Bird*. She tells the story of her father helping her brother write a school essay on birds: "Bird by bird, buddy. Just take it bird by bird."

"Do you remember those old manuals IBM used to put out with their software?" I'm sitting by a fire at a retreat center with my longtime friend, the wonderful author Seth Godin, and he's giving me advice on how to keep going when you want to give up. "When you're stuck, you should just do what they did . . . stick a blank page in the stuck point and type: 'This Page Left Intentionally Blank.'"

Bird by bird. Blank page by blank page. Ridge by ridge. Step by step. And, if need be, do-over after do-over after do-over—tacking across the surface of the lake, of your life, of the book you've promised to write, the friend's journey you've promised to complete, making incremental progress that's directionally correct.

ASTEROID STRIKES AND STRATEGIC RETREATS

So, we move across the lake, this way and that. We launch a business and we think, *Ah, I'm in the search business*, and suddenly some tool we created to make our business run more smoothly is seen by a customer who says, "Wait, I don't want your product, I want *that*." And you shift, your business is different.

Or sometimes, in moving across the lake, you major in English in college and, finally, you've got an answer to the question your sister asked you on Flatbush Avenue all those years later: I'm going to be a teacher, like you.

But then, suddenly, you're in your adviser's office, crying about the fact that you don't have the money for tuition and that you must drop out, and Professor Robert Greenberg says, Well, that's not going to happen. You're not dropping out. I'm the judge of a scholarship contest and I'm going to give you the scholarship. It'll pay your tuition until you finish up.

An asteroid strike—you can stay in school and then you tack in a completely different direction because the scholarship comes with a summer internship.

A few months later you're spending your summer proofreading copy at a weekly technology magazine and unbeknownst to you, you've stumbled into a career that will eventually lead to a position as an investor in technology companies and, still later, as a coach, talking with folks about their own twisty, topsy-turvy lives.

Like the award-winning filmmaker and entrepreneur Jeff Orlowski. You leave high school thinking you're going to be a professional photographer, a professional cyclist, or a professional pianist—certainly not an engineer, as your mother wanted. So, yes, you agree to go to Stanford, and then one day you see a notice that a climate scientist needs an assistant to help take pictures, and as a web-savvy teenager you're using your skills to launch a business that builds websites for photographers like your father. And through that connection you find out that a climate scientist needs a website built, and, hey, you know how to do that, so you offer to do some free work, and months later, you're in Greenland, setting up cameras to photograph. And years later, your new friends have made a film that picks up awards at festivals around the world and you find yourself onstage with close friends accepting an Emmy.

And suddenly you're a filmmaker. What's more, you're an entrepreneur, raising money, making product-art to change the world.

"Um, so I went to a camp," Jeff told me. "I went to a camp when I was in high school called Camp Rising Sun. It's this youth leadership program in upstate New York. It had a profound impact on me for . . . for countless reasons." And he tells me a story about the campfires held every Saturday night.

Teenagers, youth leaders all, sitting around the fire, thinking, "What shall I do with my life?" Some think, "Professional cyclist, photographer, or pianist." Others are even less sure.

"The elders in the community would share some insights, some wisdom," he continued. "There was one that a friend of mine, a mentor, gave that has stuck with me for a really, really long time." The mentor, Chris, was a skilled chess player and he'd drawn some analogies between chess and life. "He shared this concept of a strategic retreat." There are times both in chess and in life, when you're going down a certain path, and you hit a roadblock. And then you realize that the moves you're trying to make aren't working out. "At those times, I have to abandon that game plan and re-strategize, and make a strategic retreat and take a different plan of attack."

I pointed out that the retreat is strategic because it's smart, it keeps you safe, and it comes from a place of being brave enough to admit that you need to choose differently. That the path isn't straight and up and to the right.

We can't plan for an asteroid strike. As I learned lying on the banks of the Colorado, at the bottom of the canyon, the best we can do is relax our gaze and let the shooting stars streak across our life.

WHAT STOPS YOU FROM HAVING THE LIFE YOU DESERVE?

I'm racing to make a flight when my cell phone vibrates. Fuck. Who's calling now? I look down at the LCD, pre-smartphone screen—this is 1996—it's Mark Pincus.

Fuck. Mark is calling me again. Months before, I'd met Mark and his partner, Sunil Paul, when they were raising money for their first start-up, Freeloader. Sunil and I had known each other from my days at CMP and we continued to stay in touch after I left CMP and helped start CMG@Ventures, a tiny-venture fund that was part of a public company called CMG Inc. (CMGI).

Mark knew an investor, Fred Wilson, then with a venture firm called Euclid Partners. Fred invested in Freeloader. I couldn't get the deal past my partners. Even though I was not an investor, I continued to respond to Mark's requests for help.

"Jerry," he'd e-mail, "what do you think of this revenue model?" I delighted in Mark despite his relentlessness.

Racing to board my flight, I choose to answer my phone. *Bam*, another asteroid strikes. My path suddenly altered, and here is a new, unexpected way forward.

"Fred's raising a new fund," Mark blurts out, "and you should be his partner."

Six months or so later, we'd launched Flatiron Partners.

What if I hadn't taken his call? What if I had simply followed my initial, selfish impulses and ignored Mark's insistent, incessant, requests for help—"Dammit, I'm not even an investor. I have nothing to gain from helping you."

What if I hadn't walked into Professor Greenberg's office and admitted that I'd been ignoring the letters from the bursar's office?

Since then, I've passed through the Flatiron days, I've floated down the Colorado River, lived through the crazy-making experiences of sudden-wealth syndrome and shame-producing consequences of businesses I've invested in failing, and years later, I've emerged, scarred but steady. Alive and thriving.

I'm on my own, working as a coach. Fred's still a close friend as is Brad Feld, another loving asteroid in my life whom I first met in the early days of my career, back when we all had thick black hair and laughing enthusiasm for the sheer fun of building a new world out of this thing called the Internet.

Both Fred and Brad love me and are generous and kind in singing my praises. I can take in some of their love and yet I know, too, that it's coming through the filter of decades of friendship.

One day, an e-mail arrives. "I was reading a blog post by Fred Wilson," wrote Khalid Halim. In the post, he'd written that I was the best CEO coach he knew. Khalid explained that he wanted to be a coach and wondered if I would be willing to help him.

At that point, I was overwhelmed. "I don't have time for

another client," I said to myself petulantly. My old, old, old sense of too many people wanting too much from me rises. Yet the sincerity of his wish stops me, and I read his note again and again. He wants to help others, I see. I think I see his heart. I say yes to an early-Saturday-morning call, every few weeks.

And yet today, he's one of my partners in this heart-filled enterprise where we take closed, scared, and scarred leaders and help their hearts break open and for warriors to emerge.

There's Khalid, with whom I partnered to form Reboot. There's Dan Putt, another former client turned partner and co-founder whose strength and gentleness were clear to me even as they were shielded from him, shielded by the confusion of his self-doubt and his rigidly held belief that there was a path to entrepreneurial freedom, nirvana, and life everlasting. His own capacity was blocked by the firmly held belief that the reason he couldn't see the path clearly was that he was broken. Not that the path is pathless but that he wasn't worthy to trod it.

And Ali Schultz, our fourth co-founder, herself an asteroid with a sparkly smile and fierce heart who challenged me to step into my own capacity with her own simple question on a walk in the hills surrounding Boulder: "What stops you from building the life you really deserve?"

What if I hadn't answered that e-mail from Khalid? The request for coaching from Dan? Or the invitation from Ali to hike? What if I hadn't put Dan together with Khalid together with Ali and all three challenged the four of us to take the next step and build a company out of the singular lives we'd crafted for ourselves?

One day, long after having given up his dream of being a

writer—the unspoken, unacknowledged answer to his sister Mary's question of what he'd like to be when he grew up, the unvoiced plan behind his wish to be remembered—the English major turned tech reporter turned venture capitalist turned brokenhearted coach, got an e-mail from a prestigious editor from a prestigious publisher: Have you ever considered writing a book? One day, I had the courage to answer an e-mail that would have me writing a chapter on the life transformations of asteroid strikes and how purpose is lived into and not merely found.

Sometimes the paralysis of choice stems not from the path being winding, unpredictable, and uncertain but from the forks in the road. Implicit in the belief that the path is not, in fact, pathless is the belief that there's a wrong fork and, worse, we may choose unwisely, only to regret our lives.

It's hard enough to fend off the fear of choosing unwisely. It's hard enough to try to relax your gaze enough to know that life will unfold however it will unfold and somehow just be okay with that. Harder still is the burden of disappointing those who wish us to step off onto one fork or the other.

Sage Joseph Campbell, with love and joy, suggested we follow our bliss. But when facing that fork in the road, when at the crossroad, choosing to tack left or right, we want so much to know which path will lead to bliss.

If we knew which path the right path was, crossroads wouldn't be as mystical or magical as they are.

"Look for the turtles," I said one day to then-client Dan Putt while he sat on my couch, wondering which fork to take. "Look for the turtles," I said, thinking it made me sound like a wise old soul. "Look for the turtles," I said, recalling the joy-filled instructions his late mother would share with him as they would wander for a walk at a nearby pond during the latter stages of her battle with breast cancer.

How do you look for the turtles when you're unsure which path the turtles are taking? How do you even know where to look for the turtles?

That is this life's work because that is the work of our lives. Like Dan and so many others like me, sitting on the couch listening to Ani Pema speak of the pathless path, we often suffer because we are convinced that the path to fulfillment and a life of purpose is out there to be discovered, found. Once found (or pointed to by some wise sage), our task—we believe—is to head out, unflinchingly, striding with clear-eyed resolve.

We come of age asking ourselves, "Who am I to be?" Later, as we live our way into being who we are, we come to questions, "What am I to do?" and "What is my purpose?" Later still, as our elder-wisdom seeps into our bones, we might replace that question with the simple "Have I been kind?"

Am I the adult I was supposed to be when, under the boardwalk, I shook my fist at the sky and declared that this was not to be my life? Is *this* the life of meaning that is my birthright?

There's a devilish trap, though, in that question. A trap exacerbated by the admonitions and advice of writers, ascetics, sages, and charlatans who overtly or covertly offer steps on the path. The trap is implicit in the question: Purpose is not something external to us. It's not a place to get to. The admonitions, instructions, and advice of others will, at best, fall short and, at worst, make one feel nothing but harshly self-critical for even holding the question in the first place.

The wise teacher Joseph Campbell wrote that people conflate the pursuit of purpose with a pursuit of aliveness. I'll go further, though; aliveness comes not from having magically discovered purpose, meaning, nirvana, and a never-ending supply of lemon drops.

Aliveness comes from living a life of personal integrity in which our outer actions match our inner values, beliefs, wishes, and dreams. I am living my purpose, living with aliveness, when I write, regardless of whether my words are published. This then defines our life's work not as a path to be discovered (and certainly not by following someone else's map) but as a way of being, where each day is a chance to live into the command to live with the inner and outer in alignment. Acknowledging the days, weeks, months, and years when we have not lived that way, giving ourselves the do-over, the freshness of beginner's mind, to rise again and try again.

Work—our careers, our professions, our jobs—is neither the blissful expression of deep purpose nor the dreadful obligation that stands in the way of being ourselves. Work is an opportunity for a daily realignment of the inner and outer, a daily do-over of life expressed with integrity.

Transformation is not how we discover the path up and to the right. No matter how many trips around Wonderland Lake we take, we are still bound to the truest task: live into congruency, tacking across the lake where the winds powering us are the answers to the questions. Who are we? What do we believe to be true, today? What is the world we wish to create every day with our actions and our hearts?

This calling to a deep, radical inquiry into self is not only the path of transformation, the path to purpose but, in the end, how we grow strong, resilient, and capable of meeting the world like the openhearted warriors we were born to be. By this process of withstanding the asteroid strikes of people, of loss, of confusion, we fill the holes in our chests not with marionettes, cars, or even money but with our own souls. We turn the wounds of every day into sacred and healing balms for others and for ourselves. We must therefore remain open to those asteroids and the smart, strategic retreats.

Standing still; leaning in; and listening to our children, our partners, our loves, our employees, our customers, and, most important, our own hearts—that is how we grow.

Walking the forests, canyons, and trails of life, I marvel at split boulders. How does something so substantive, so strong, split in half? The boulder splits because over eons, drip by drip, water carves out first an indentation, then a divot, then a depression, until a pool forms, turns to ice, expands, and splits the rock.

We are the rock. Our splits occur after the drip, drip, drip becomes a pool and the cold freezes the water, creating pressure strong enough to break us open. This is how we grow. We integrate the asteroid strikes, the twists and turns of forks in the road. The pain of uncertainty, missteps, strategic retreats, the echoing voices in our heads that caution us to choose wisely.

Then, suddenly, the rock splits, air rushes in, the next few steps on a path become clear, and we stride forward. Although we are unsure of what it will all lead to, everything nevertheless becomes purposeful. Everything becomes sacred when good work is done well for the right reasons.

The drama of being human is great and complicated. The pathless path is pockmarked with pain and suffering. But seen from the vantage point that all steps are purposeful, all of it becomes worthwhile—a glorious, life-giving retort to those who would question our worthiness and lovability.

Journaling Invitations

What's my purpose?

———————

Why do I feel lost while I struggle to move forward?

———————

How do I grow, transform, and build a life of meaning?

CHAPTER 7

———————

Loving the Crow

It took years, but I finally learned to love the whole of me and become a warrior. It's been quite a journey.

As a teenager, I found something romantic and noble about the writer who throws his manuscript into the fireplace or the painter who, in a fit of self-loathing, slashes her finished work with a razor.

In my thirties, I began to map out the web that links my most critical inner voices and, perversely, my persistent wishes for love, safety, and belonging. Moreover, I began to see how each of our inner loves, conflicts, and lives is projected into the world through our relationships, our companies, and our work. Only now, in my fifties, have I begun to realize that those critical voices—the ones whispering that we are no good, *less than*, a fake—are, ironically, meant to soothe us and keep us safe. The voice of the inner critic is meant to protect us from humiliation and shame, from the risks of being found out—from being seen as the impostor, the charlatan, we fear we may be—or think we already know we are.

HATING THE LIFE WE'VE CREATED

"I hate the fucking product," said Maria, my client. She has curled her body into the corner of the pale blue couch in my office, hugging one of the two burnt-orange pillows, the one with a small black ink stain. I stared at the stain and my mind drifted to movies and books filled with scenes of the angst-ridden artist. "I wake, grab the app, and feel sick," she continued. "I want to tear everything apart and start all over."

I know that pain. I reminded myself that existential lacerations can feel more painful than bodily pain. When I was the editor of *InformationWeek* magazine, we worked for months on a redesign; we had hours-long conversations about every meticulous detail. We debated font size, picas, and kerning. We compared color scheme after color scheme. When we were done, I felt a rush of pride as the first copies came back from the printer.

A month later, I hated everything about that damn new design.

Why do we hate what we labor so long to create?

It's partly because neither the song we hear in our head nor the application we dream up late at night as we can't sleep, nor the story we write in the car as we drive home, nor the company we quit our safe job to found is ever the same as the song that's eventually sung. It pains me when I see my clients, artists every one of them, frustrated that no one can hear the notes as well as they can.

I think of Drew, who's burned through CTO after CTO, firing one after another. "Make it like this," I imagine him saying as he races across the whiteboard, making everyone slightly nauseated with the fumes of the markers. "Then it should do this, then this, and then this . . ." Make the users feel this way; and then that . . . or that. And inevitably they blurt out: "No, no, no. NOT that," grabbing the dry-erase marker, " . . . like this!"

I see the product manager shake his head and the engineer slinking back to her desk, muttering to each other, "What the hell does he want now?!?"

Sometimes our frustration grows out of boredom—familiarity breeding contempt. We live with our creations, day in, day out, and come to hate them. Seeing only the flaws in the creation, we're simply, painfully facing our deepest insecurities, our deepest doubts about our right to create anything at all.

Most important, though, the frustration is egged on by a whispery, persistent, critical voice asking, "Who the hell do you think you are, as if you could cause this impossible, glorious song to come into being? Why would anyone want to use something you created? You're just wrong. Everyone knows you've no idea what you're doing."

I feel it most acutely when I write. Some days, I hate every single syllable I type. I even hate that sentence. This one, too.

I took a few writing courses in college. One professor, the brilliant poet Marie Ponsot, would talk about the Crow sitting on your shoulder saying things like: "That sucks," "How could you write that?" and "Are you kidding me?!?" Diminutive, chain-smoking Marie would raise her tobacco-stained fingers into the air, punctuating every word: "Shoot. The. Damn. Crow."

Each time our work fails to live up to our whispered expectations (or those grumblings we convince ourselves might be held against us by our employees, our investors, our colleagues, and our loved ones), we're reminded of one of our most complicated and intricate fearful belief systems: We will inevitably fail because we are a fraud; and such failure will prove, once and for all, what we suspected all along—that we are unworthy of love, do not belong anywhere, and are, therefore, wholly unsafe.

These everyday failures become evidence that we are not only unsafe but undeserving of even *wishing* for safety at all. The Crow, after cawing into our ear about our failure and our fraudulent true self, hops to the other shoulder, cawing that we never belonged at all. The vulnerable child in each of us gets caught between the urge to be himself and the fear that doing so will bring shame and humiliation. The temptation to stay unseen (and, thus, safe) is strong. *Caw-caw-caw.*

If you succeed in being your own self, and bringing forth your own creations, you run the risk of humiliating rejection. The cawing admonishes: Don't create; don't express who you are truly.

The pain of hating our own creation is a consequence of our investing too much of our sense of being into the company, the product, the creation. When we hang our sense of self on the whisper of an idea; when we unwittingly insist that our love, safety, and belonging depend on what we do and, most important, how *others* feel about our feelings, our actions, and our work; then we leave little space for anything other than bitter, existential suffering.

LIFE IN THE SHADOW

As Carl Jung notes, "Until you make the unconscious conscious, it will direct your life and you will call it fate." Jung goes on to assert that humans place the positive and negative attributes of our character—our feelings, beliefs, the things we typically define as strengths and weaknesses; anything that conflicts with our sense of who and what we are supposed to be—into our personal shadow. This allegorical shadow operates the way our true shadow does—behind us, just out of our direct sight, where we have but the vaguest awareness of its existence. We glimpse it only by craning our necks.

Collectively, those qualities and aspects that are incompatible with our sense of who we *need* to be to be loved and to belong get rejected, disowned, and placed in an unlit, unseen part of our consciousness; forever denied and angrily, anxiously, guiltily defended against.

These attributes continue to exist, marinating in our lived experiences, brewing into a cocktail potent enough to knock us and those we cherish onto our asses. In being denied, these attributes grow in intensity; periodically, explosively, often tragically, these attributes step out of the shadow and into the scenes of our lives in troubling and troublesome ways.

There's the leader whose childhood was marked by poverty and deprivation and, in a bid to feel safe, nurses ambition and desperate cravings to prove all the doubters wrong. But, given the strictures of their childhood or family structures, given the risk of expulsion from the only tribe they may ever have known, they bury that ambition, labeling the wish for money as "greed" and placing it out of sight, in their shadow, over their shoulder, into what the poet Robert Bly dubbed the "long black bag" we drag behind us.

Or the CEO whose brilliant ways threatened her standing in middle school, and so, more than merely denying her intellect, she actively rejects any challenging books or squirms in a classroom seat, lest her light be revealed, her artistry manifested, and her place in the family threatened. Unconsciously she internalizes the isolation caused by the middle-school bullies, remaining cut off from potential allies and isolated from colleagues.

All of it—all the positive, all the negative aspects of our character that make us stand out, be different—is thrown into that long black bag.

Just as shooting stars are best glimpsed peripherally, we must rely on others to help us see how our disowned positive and negative attributes are determining our conscious lives. Recently I sat in my current therapist's office, his chair across from mine, lamenting again about the unfair and inexplicable aspects of my life. Again and again, I lay out in fine detail all the ways I've been wronged.

At such times, my rage drives an intense plotting and scheming. I think about the moves and countermoves I'd make in the battle with that other person.

"Do you see it?" my therapist asks. "Do you see that the more you plot, the cleverer you feel? And the cleverer you feel, the more hooked on the anger you become? You nurse and feed that anger until you're operating purely out of your shadow."

I look up startled, ashamed, feeling caught with my true feelings—my anger—revealed. My oh-so-clever facade of brilliant plotting and analysis was laid bare.

There's only one way we can know if our disowned selves are calling the shots. We must take the radical step of inquiring into our selves, seeking to see ourselves with clarity, grace, compassion, and a fierce commitment to cut through our own bullshit. We open ourselves up to ways we've been complicit in creating the conditions we say we don't want.

We check, for example, the patterns of our lives. Why do we always hire greedy salespeople? Why do we always find ourselves feeling annihilated by and subordinate to those with more structural power? And, more telling, when does our typical pattern of equanimity get so quickly and readily disturbed? Despite having worked so hard to learn the quality and beauty of standing still, why do I still lie awake at night, again and again, nursing the same old injuries and perceived slights? Clients, friends, and I—each of us, all of us—can lament: "Fuck my life. Why does this always happen to me?"

Worse still, because our denied attributes live just outside our daily view, our conscious mind is convinced the consequences of that denial of self must come from some outside force. It is not *my denial* of the totality of who I am that causes me distress; it's always the Irrational Other.

The key to understanding is noticing the reaction. Dr. Sayres, my once-longtime therapist, would say, "If it's hysterical, it's historical." If there's an outsized reaction—negative or positive—chances are you're operating from your shadow. Or, even more precisely, grabbing an attribute out of the long black bag and flinging it onto the people in your life and blaming them for your internal discontent.

Of course, it takes some skill to unpack the black bag. We're remarkably skilled at dodging and weaving, protecting the unseen things from the light of day. When a client begins to unpack such patterns, the Crow will flap his wings, cock his head, and turn his jet-black eye toward a juicy bit of self-revelation and twist it into further self-criticism. "See?!" he'll croak into my client's ear. "We knew you were essentially a shit."

One of the Crow's many trickster defenses is to see the radical self-inquiry process as an inquisition. Seeing the look in their eye, recognizing the audible gulp that signals a recognition, I'll joke about the ways in which we all do this. "This isn't evidence of your unlovability," I'll interject, disrupting the inquiry-into-inquisition process. "It's evidence of your humanity."

More important, I explain, it's proof that you learned the most important skill any human needs: survival.

THE LOYAL SOLDIER AND SURVIVING INTO ADULTHOOD

I first read of the Loyal Soldier on my way back from Greenland. I've never been sure why I went to Greenland in the first place. It was during my post–JPMorgan years, my years of learning to sit, learning to listen to my own heart, so perhaps that process led to a restlessness and a desire to feel the Earth more viscerally.

I went with an adventurous plan: spend two weeks on a peninsula on the East Coast, experience life in a polar region. Skiing and trekking 200 kilometers and camping every night (or whatever there was of "night" at that latitude in April).

The first night, we pitched our tent on thousand-year-old ice, more than a mile thick. The sun was bright, even though it was ten o'clock. We'd traveled for more than five hours by snowmobile from a tiny airstrip near Scoresby Sund, a fjord system on the southeastern corner of Greenland.

We crawled into our tents, excited and tired. Hours passed. A dusky night sky replaced the bright-as-day light. I lay in my sleeping bag, wrapped in my down jacket, pants, booties, and more clothes than I'd ever worn at one time before. I stared at a thermometer hanging from the top of the tent's interior. I watched the tiny sliver of mercury drop from a warm twenty degrees Fahrenheit to well below zero. Within days, I'd had a bad fall, busted up my hip and, far sooner than I expected, I was back on a plane, first to Iceland and then home.

It was on that trip home that I read depth psychologist Bill Plotkin's *Soulcraft* and recognized my Loyal Soldier, who'd dedicated his life to saving me from being cast out, keeping me safe, and making me feel loved.

The image is poignantly simple. A lone soldier, cut off from the rest of his comrades, defending an isolated rock of an island, armed with just an old rifle. The soldiers have had no contact with the outside world for months, for years. They have eaten only elk, as the poet Robert Bly would write, avoided elevators, and made up their minds to "save you from death." Alone, cut off, convinced that the war they signed up to fight is still raging at home, they swear to defend this rock, this piece of the homeland, by oiling their rifle, keeping up their routines, and drilling themselves in the rules that will keep you safe. These include rules such as this: Stay small. Don't stand out. Careful now. Don't make mistakes.

The rules, these Loyal Survival Strategies, show up throughout our lives, morphing and weaving into each other. For one person, it may be the admonition to *always put others before oneself*. That's a problem, of course, when such movement isn't rooted in a healthy, life-giving altruism but stems, instead, from the belief that anything but the total negation of the self risks incurring the wrath of those around us—those charged with keeping us well and whole. For another, though, it might be to *always put yourself first*, lest you'll be left with nothing but scraps from the family dinner.

At our boot camps, when we talk of the Loyal Soldier, a hush tends to fall over the group as the campers slowly recognize aspects of their own lives, their ways of being. Tears begin to flow when they realize that these aspects were necessary for their love, safety, and belonging—their very survival. One camper comes to recognize that his codependent caretaking and incessant need to save and fix—behavior so rewarded on his path to leadership—may be rooted in a childhood fixation that, if he were to advance his own wishes, his mother would make good on her persistent threats to leave. Another may come to see that being a "perky people person" is an inauthentic effort (but nevertheless admirable and honorable) to contain Dad's rage and the threat of violence. For some, the strategies may lie behind the need to avoid conflict. Or, for another, the belief that being alone, alone with one's thoughts, is dangerous. "Don't look there," I imagine hearing a soldier warn my client. "Let sleeping dogs lie." Each time I glimpse a survival strategy, I hear the slide, click, slam, of a bolt-action rifle, as if the Loyal Soldier were readying her weapon, looking across the sea toward home, and saying, "Don't worry, I've got this. I'll keep you loved, safe, and right where you belong."

For many, that place where we've come to *think* we belong has become stultifying; it's where we are small, unseen, unsure, and unwilling to claim our strengths, our capacities, our courage, our leadership. We are frozen by the belief that it's just too dangerous to reach into the black bag and grab hold of the disowned, dismembered parts of ourselves.

All Loyal Soldiers then have one basic task: to keep us safe from the wars that raged in our childhood. No matter how awful these strategies have come to make us feel as adults, they were brilliant in their own ways.

I know that to be true because I see you. I see that you are here, that you are, despite feeling broken and inadequate, an adult who's fully capable of loving and being loved, of being safe and keeping others safe, and belonging. You survived.

You've grown into an adult, capable of grasping the ways these successful survival strategies outlived their usefulness. Your Loyal Soldiers did a fine job. They just don't know the war is over.

While the Crow may pester us, he loves us and wants to keep us safe from the pain of humiliation. And for these reasons, I welcome home my beautiful, proud, vigilant Loyal Soldiers and thank my Crow for the gifts he's placed at my feet.

THE GIFTS FROM THE CROW

The flight from Reykjavik to New York crossed Newfoundland; my hip hurt, and I was relieved to be headed home. Glimpsing the landmass of North America, I thought of the Vikings: "I'll bet it's easier to get to North America now than it was back then."

As I stared out the jet's window, my mind wandered from random thoughts of Vikings to icy lands called "green" and green lands called "ice." My Crow then woke up and went to work. "Why did you leave the expedition early? You could have made it all the way to the end. So your hip got hurt? What's wrong with you? You always do this, you always start something but never finish it . . ."

Staring at the blackness of the North Atlantic, trying to catch glimpses of icebergs, tears welled up as I listened to my Crow: "What is wrong with you? You know . . . if I've told you once, I've told you a million times, you're not the man people think you are. You're not the man you pretend to be."

Sitting on the plane, making my way back to my life, my family, in pain, the best my mind could muster was additional harsh self-criticism.

A decade later, I see how the self-criticism of the Crow and the defensiveness of the Loyal Soldier have been essential, helping me survive my life. I see them as gifts, but not ones that can't be put down and left behind.

Harsh self-criticism? Check. I live with daily questions as to whether I'm a good enough man, father, life and business partner, and leader. Indeed, listening to my own heart more closely, I hear the five-year-old in me making sense of the world: Were I to be "enough"—a good enough man, parent, leader—then I might not belong to a family in which the parents daily expressed their brokenhearted pain through mental illnesses such as schizophrenia and alcoholism.

The self-criticism can be expressed in many ways but the most dominant seems to be a lacerating guilt, as my Buddhist teacher, Sharon Salzberg, describes it. With the guilt is a terror that comes from believing not merely that I'm unworthy but, in fact, have committed terrible, terrible sins.

Indeed, if I stopped worrying about this, if I let down my hypervigilant guard long enough to feel that I were enough, then I might abandon my brokenhearted parents, leaving them bereft. By leaving open the question of my worthiness, the Crow enables me to remain my parents' son.

From that one essential question, "Am I worthy enough?" flows a host of other strategies, each designed to keep me safe. Codependent caretaking, for example, whereby I struggle nobly, silently, passive-aggressively, relating to others in the vain wish that they would give me what I would want; I'd send flowers when what I wanted was to receive them.

Or a pleasing persona—in my case, the happy, all-knowing Buddhist who secretly is capable of mowing down any who oppose him, sometimes with angry brute force but more often with a stealthy stiletto.

As I grew into adulthood, I used my vigilance to read a room. As a reporter, I used this sensitivity to persuade interviewees to reveal things that no one else could get them to reveal. As an investor, I relied on these gifts to grok the entrepreneurs' deepest motivations and understand intuitively the best ways to partner with them. Years later, as a coach, I use my Crow's gifts to help my clients listen to their own hearts.

Indeed, every survival strategy—every whispered warning from our ever-on-guard Loyal Soldiers and the Crows of our lives, carry remarkable gifts. My need to please, for example, became a life-affirming, life-giving dedication to being of genuine service to others. Similarly, my need to be seen as calm, calming, mature, and capable became a lasting skill with which I can be, in fact, capable and competent, and a calming influence, even during a raging storm.

The need to be perceived as good enough to be loved led me—indeed, continues to compel me—to see every dip and ascension of this roller coaster called life as a means for inner exploration and outer growth. The habits birthed in a fearful wish to be loved, to be safe, and to belong became the structures of my adulthood and how I can help others feel loved, safe, and that they belong.

There's a gift, even in the most painful whispered warning: "If they only knew the real me . . . they'd see how incompetent, screwed up, broken, angry I really am. If they really saw through my masks, they'd see the awful things I've done. And if they saw those things, I'd be thrust out of the tribe, bereft; left to die alone, cold, unloved, and deeply, deeply ashamed."

The gift is often hard to see and is just as often misread. It is not what my clients who struggle with their own versions of the impostor syndrome believe it to be. It is not the source of some sort of "driver," a guard against complacency, that will compel them to excellence.

Such a belief is yet another crafty whispered warning from a Loyal Soldier. Such a warning is false, because implicit in the warning is the fundamental belief that behind it all, we are lazy, good-for-nothing slackers who seek nothing more than to be complacent, giving up authorship of our own lives. Nothing can be more false.

The Buddha taught that because we are born human, we are inherently, basically good. Far from being lazy slackers, we are born with wishes, dreams, and the desire to live in tribes with love, safety, and belonging.

"WHO HERE IS BRAVE ENOUGH TO ADMIT THEY'RE TERRIFIED?"

I paced the stage in front of the gathered large audience of mostly first-time CEOs. The stage was at a convention center in San Francisco. As I often do, I paused to let the crowd settle down, settle into their bodies. I'd already made a few people laugh by kicking off my shoes, explaining to the front row that my feet are so big that my shoes feel heavy and I need to be light.

The talk was on the challenge of leadership. I begin with two questions:

"Who here is brave enough to admit they are terrified?" And, "Who's smart enough to admit they haven't a clue about how to do their job?"

Everyone laughs. Everyone relaxes. One gift that emerges from radical self-inquiry is the recognition that the whole system is rigged. That only those with extreme mental well-being or those with an extreme mental disorder are unbothered by such doubts.

When we're brave enough to admit our fears, uncertainties, and doubts, we open the gift box. Putting aside the bright wrapping paper and ribbons our Loyal Soldier has carefully assembled, we extract the ability to accept our humanity, our flaws, the wholeness of our selves. Then, in opening to our humanity, we open to the glorious, wondrous gift of our shared humanity. "Oh," we exclaim, "you feel broken, too? Awesome, let's be human together."

In loving the gifts of the Crow, we end up negating the very threat about which he warned. Our soldier, so desperate to make sure we don't end up alone, told us over and over to hide our doubts. By admitting our doubts, we get to enjoy one of the great gifts of being human: belonging.

In loving his gifts, I learned to love my Crow. In loving my Crow, I've begun the painful work of retrieving the parts of me from my black bag. The act of leading and the art of growing up depend on each of us, finally, eventually, repeatedly sorting the unsorted baggage we've been traveling with since childhood.

THE UNSORTED BAGGAGE OF LEADERSHIP

For those who hold power, the price of unsorted baggage is paid by those with whom they pass their days—their coworkers, peers, direct reports. Of course, not all organizational challenges can be traced back to the dismembered, unsorted parts of themselves in the leaders' shadows. But the toughest, most intransigent, most troubling aspects of the collective unconscious blithely referred to as culture can more effectively be worked when the leader commits to doing self-inquiry work. Power in the hands of one afraid or unwilling to look in the mirror perpetuates an often silent, always seething violence in the workplace. Worse still, when a leader leads from his or her shadow, the dismembering havoc is perpetuated down the line until the company, the tribe, the community simply assumes this is how life must be.

I was called to lead an off-site with a senior leadership team. The problem on the table, the "presenting agenda" to use a coaching term, was that the company was "stuck," and the CEO and the board were frustrated by the lack of innovation and progress.

The morning we were to start the off-site, the CEO pulled me aside: both the heads of sales and engineering had called in sick. This was a problem, because each of them was considered a problem. Everyone else had already concluded that the aggressive style each of them showed was the reason the company couldn't make any decisions.

"I don't think either of them is really sick," the CEO confided in me. "I think they just don't want to deal with all the touchy-feely stuff you make people talk about." I nodded and joked about having a pheromone that makes people cry.

We began by talking about the ways we listen and the ways we do—or don't—communicate. I asked about how failure was handled. I listened with my head, my ears, but then listened with my body as well. My head was pleased. It all sounded right.

"We celebrate failure," someone offered. I smiled, made small talk about failure and mistakes. Again, it all sounded right.

But my body felt otherwise, and my vigilant heart perked up. "How do you handle disagreement?" They looked puzzled and stayed silent. I pressed on. "I mean, you've more than a thousand employees now, you've got to disagree sometime. Do you celebrate that?" More silence.

Following my intuition, I wandered over to the CEO. "Tell me how disagreement was handled in your family," I asked, echoing the work I did with the other, conflict-avoidant team. "Was there any violence at home?"

Shocked, he said emphatically, "No! Not at all." Puzzled, I turned away, listening to my gut. The CEO added quickly, "Only a lot of yelling."

I smiled, putting a question to the whole room, "Does anyone on your team ever yell?"

He paused before noting, "Only those two who didn't show up today."

With that one move, we quickly pieced together their unconscious, unspoken cultural rules. Conflict was to be avoided at all costs. In this case, it might lead to unacceptable yelling, which is too threatening.

The result was an incredibly loving culture to which most folks were deeply loyal. Most folks. To those for whom frustration was an inherent part of experimentation, of ambition, of drive, the culture was to be fought against at every turn.

Experimentation creates tension. It carries a risk of failure. Moreover, when such experiments succeed, and companies innovate, people have to integrate change. The potential of failure and the need for change can terrify people. It can feel like the conflicts from their childhood that folks were programmed to avoid.

Then those who clearly see the need for change in an organization become the unconscious holders of the tension. The frustrations that drove the company to try to change and innovate get banished. The falsely safe and loving culture is preserved but the company slowly strangles itself with a lack of new ideas and an inability to confront competitors.

When the leader is willing to embrace that which has been banished—to embrace without fear the potential of failure, for example—then a company is able to free itself from the false safety of conflict avoidance and change and grow.

Or consider Julie. Her pitches to investors were always perfect, and she was on her way to building a killer company, one destined—I predicted—to radically disrupt the ways economically disadvantaged people received high-quality food.

As part of her preparations, she'd blast music from the

nineties to rev herself up. Yet often the deal making would snag. She'd get the yes on the merits of the deal—the strong underlying economics of the company and the compelling arguments about the return on investment. But often she'd struggle to close the transaction. Worse still, once closed, the investors would often end up in an adversarial stance. The Crow on her shoulder would sit up, stretch its wings, and cock an eye, looking for signs of trouble.

Then, one day, really by accident, she heard a story from another CEO who related that before *her* pitch meetings, she'd stand still; she'd sit in meditation. She'd go back to an insight she'd gained at one of our camps about the deeply held reason why she launched the business in the first place.

The next day, Julie found herself uninterested in the nineties pop she'd regularly listened to. Instead, she just sat. As she sat, she remembered. She remembered the ways her parents struggled to pay the bills; she pulled in the fear and the shame that the family's economic challenges had induced in her. She wept, and through the tears she saw the seven-year-old version of herself, being mocked for the crappy, unfashionable clothes she wore to school. She heard the nineties pop music in her head not as an anthem of survival but as a ballad of the pain of becoming herself.

"I cried so much," she told me. "I was scared because the meeting was only a few minutes away." But then, when she walked into the room of wealthy, powerful men, something shifted. She opened the pitch not by speaking of the amazing economic opportunity before her but with a simple declaration: "I grew up poor and I don't think poverty should stop anyone from receiving nutritious food. That's why I launched my company and that's why we should partner."

The investors were enrapt; they'd found not only a company to back but a leader to believe in.

For some, the disowned, dismembered parts of themselves show up with a fury. At the request of a friend, I'd begun working with a new client. Patrick's lead investor said, "He's a little rough around the edges but he could really use your help." After a few conversations, Patrick and I agreed to start the engagement with a performance review. We'd interview folks in his life and give him a picture of how they saw him.

"This is the worst 360-degree review I've ever seen," I said at the debriefing session. His colleagues had described him as "bullying," "toxic," "enraging," and "dismissive." Patrick had had a chance to review the report before we spoke, and he had an unexpected mix of shame and curiosity. He was not at all defensive and, in fact, shared that he felt the descriptions were accurate.

Following my intuition, I encouraged him not to disown the anger behind all that behavior. I put his mind at ease by describing how some companies thrive on intense debate. "Some companies' cultures are rock tumblers," I said. "You put dusty, dirty, roughed-up stones into the tumbler and then hours later you end up with polished jewels. The stones banging into each other forcing a positive transformation."

He loved the image. I went on, "The problem is, though, not everyone wants to work in a rock tumbler. And that's okay, too, but you may soon find yourself with no colleagues."

Instead, we explored his banished anger as if it were an old friend. He recalled story after story of being told how wrong he was for being angry and, importantly, how he'd always find some sneaky way to get back at those who "told" on him. In fact, I realized that part of the reason he wasn't defensive about the descriptions was that he was used to being called these things. In fact, he relished it; indeed, he expected me to slip into the role of the chastising parent or teacher. Just another adult telling him "bad boy" and banishing him to his room.

I refused to go along and instead said, "Well, I think you have a right to your anger. You should be pissed off, given your childhood. But the question now is, what will Patrick, the adult, choose to do with that anger?"

When Peter explored his inability to celebrate his team's success, he found his grandparents who had survived the Nazi pogroms back in Poland by staying low and out of sight, and never letting themselves be seen. In his own paranoia about his company's competitors, he found his grandparents' survival instinct embedded in their unshakable belief in the hostility of the world.

Trace the roots of a leader's boredom with a well-functioning team and the desire to shake things up, and you may find a fear of complacency that would allow the family's enemies to catch them off guard. Or explore a CEO's sexual relationship with her co-founder, and you may stumble upon a commitment to self-sabotage to ensure that she never outdoes her father.

"Just because you feel like shit," I tell client after client, "doesn't mean you are shit."

They laugh and are amused by the line. But sometimes we also allow ourselves to unpack that feeling "like shit" may in fact be old programming, ghosts in the machine, whose purpose is to ensure belonging. "What would happen?" I asked one leader. "What would happen if you let go of the belief in your fundamental brokenness?"

How would your life be if you *didn't* need to believe you were broken to feel loved?

How would the experience of your life change if you could rest and trust that life's goodness isn't always necessarily followed by calamity? How would the meat bag that is your body feel if you were to let go of the need to feel negative—about yourself, your partners, the future—and know, simply, that while sometimes bad follows good, just as often, good follows bad? How would it feel if we trusted that no matter how bad our actions, those who truly know us—know the person whom we're convinced only the Crow and our Loyal Soldier know—would love us?

Perhaps it can be that when a loved one dies suddenly, amid that grief, we will find hope and salvation. Or that when a stranger attacks us on the subway, knocks us unconscious, with blood gushing from our nose and a broken tooth lying next to our dazed head, we can awaken to marvel at the caring efficiency of a young New York City police officer as she presses the speed-dial button on your phone, the one marked, "Home." Or, amid the blood and broken bone, we feel the wise hands of an even younger emergency room nurse at Bellevue Hospital—his hands gently cradling your head as he asks if you know what year it is and the name of the president.

What would it be like if we were to stop externalizing responsibility for our inner state onto the Irrational Other? What would the experience of being in community in our organizations be like if, instead of overtly or covertly asking others to bear responsibility for giving us the feeling of love, we each assumed our worthiness as our birthright and no longer needed to twist and warp the other to suit our desperate wish to ease our sense of brokenness?

What would our organizations be like if we could drop the collective need to identify and ostracize the latest "demon"— the one who simply doesn't "get" us or our culture? How would the lives of our colleagues and, even more important, the lives our colleagues' children develop over time if we removed the Coney Island fun house mirrors of our unconscious biases and projections?

"Swim in your own lane," I often admonish a client. "When you're in the water, stay focused on the goal—your customers— and not on what the competitor is doing." Paranoia about the competitor—the nameless, faceless Other whose existence threatens our wishes and dreams—has for so long been a mantra in business. "Only the paranoid survive" has been repeated ad nauseam and for so long that few pause to question the roots of the paranoia; a Loyal Soldier firmly defending "mine" from "yours," dividing our organizations and our communities into us and them, the Irrational Others.

Few people question the ways such division of the world categorically implies that the world is hostile, and everyone in it is out to get us. Perhaps those in the other lane are merely vying for their own safety. Perhaps those in the lanes to our left and to our right are just scared, terrified that they, too, will be found out as lazy, good-for-nothing slackers.

Competition is healthy. Striving to do well is, in its way, life affirming. But what do we do to our organizations when we define ourselves by the existence of the Other? When we presume that the competitor in the lane next to ours is wrong, bad, or a threat, we are allowing our deepest fears about our own inadequacy to stand in as our "vision statement" and "strategic plan." An unintended, whispered consequence is that our colleagues—our friends down the hall with whom we built this thing, this product, this service, this company—may fear that they, too, are "them."

How will our leadership change when we see that there is no "them" and that there is only *us*? How will our communities shift if we're able to stop seeing our leaders as objects of our projections but as merely brokenhearted warriors striving to be a little bit better each day?

One founder of a high-integrity, nearly spiritual community asked in frustration why her colleagues seemed to no longer listen to her concerns despite their having been so well articulated. "Perhaps," I suggested, "they can't hear you because they're too busy listening to their idea of you." For that, too, is part of the merry-go-round of shadow and projection—especially with organizations with the highest intentions, whose collective Loyal Soldiers banish their fear-covering aggressions. We are often so programmed by old ghosts in the machine to see the leader as the epitome of all that we are not that we fail to see their failings, their flesh and blood, their feet of clay. We can't allow ourselves to see that if we prick them, they will bleed.

Such projections can be dizzying.

What if, instead of projecting the best of ourselves onto the Other, we took back that part of ourselves with love and laughter? What if, instead of projecting our banished dangerous rage onto the *Other*, we were to take it back and welcome it in? What if we saw the Other as a mirror and a pathway to our growth?

Our organizations might then turn away from the impulses to do violence to the self, the community, and the planet and toward being the means for each of us to grow up.

LOVING THE CROW AND RETRIEVING THE TREASURE

Of all the many gifts Dr. Sayres gave to me, the one I'm most grateful for comes in the form of an exasperated response to my endless worry that I was not good enough: "Oh, Jerry," she'd say, cutting me off, "you're incorrigible."

Somehow, over the years, I took that in, my Crow squawked and relaxed, and I reveled even in my incorrigibility, my basically good humanity, and loved my way past all the whispered warnings of Crows and Soldiers.

This, then, is the highest calling of the warrior-leader: to take our seats as humans and build humane companies, communities where it is gloriously safe for others to be human. The leader—the person living into the immense sky of that honorific—is called to use the gifts of inquiry to see which dragons we may be running from and which princesses we may be running toward. To notice with loving attention if we're over-indexing on either the soft, open front of the warrior or the strong back. For humane organizations are those that sit still, staying firmly in that place between the strong back of good processes, fiscal clarity, firmly held beliefs and values and the soft, open heart of wisdom, empathy, and fierce gentleness.

By taking back the projected qualities, by retrieving the treasure, we're less likely to build organizations that mimic and reinforce the wars of our childhood and more likely to build communities of belonging and emerge the adults we deserve to be. We get to become the adults we needed when we were children.

We're less likely, then, to be confused and seduced by notions of self-loathing. We're less likely to lack an understanding of why good people, ourselves included, do bad things. Despite there being so many companies striving to create cultures declaring their intent to do no evil, we see that by banishing the possibility of doing evil, we nearly ensure that evil will be done.

This path of warrior leadership isn't for the faint of heart. I laugh loudly when folks suggest that this is some sort of yoga-inspired soft-bellied call to leadership. "Namaste my ass," I say with my Brooklyn-born chip firmly, squarely, and proudly on my shoulder. "Try entering the cave, walking to the dark recesses, and retrieving the treasure wa-a-a-y in the back. Then come tell me about being soft."

Long ago, in response to dreadful migraines I'd developed as a child, Dr. Sayres taught me the first of three magical questions: "What am I not saying that needs to be said?" Consider that question alone when you consider your own wayward, twisting, tacking-across-the-surface-of-the-lake path to leadership and adulthood.

What have I not been saying, recently, in the last few years, in all my life, that needs and needed to be said? Consider and check your heart rate. That beat, beat, beat you feel is not love but the dread felt at approaching fierce, fearful truth.

Consider the ways the unsorted baggage of your life has

kept you from not only speaking but being heard: What am I saying that's not being heard? Consider how you've silently seethed, waiting to manipulate the team to prove that you were right all along.

Consider the ghosts in your machine, the click, click of the bolt-action rifle warning you of the dangers of truly listening to those with whom you share this Earth, this journey: What's being said that I'm not hearing? What is it that the people whom I love, the people I work with, the people who populate the stories of my life are saying that I just can't bear to hear? Is it perhaps that I have hurt them, disappointed them, or threatened their safety? Can I consider that my refusal to hear them—regardless of their chosen method of communication—furthers that pain?

Consider these things and tell me again how this path of leadership is soft.

The commitment to sort the unsorted baggage turns leadership into a journey of self-actualization. With that, work becomes not the impediment to our lives, not the repeated manifestation of our inner self-loathing, not the thing that gets in the way, but the way we can live out our lives as they were meant to be. As the poet John O'Donohue wishes for each of us, "May leadership be for you / A true adventure of growth."

Such inner work creates alignment, and alignment strengthens purpose and meaning. Welcoming home the Loyal Soldier and loving the Crow release us from the lacerations of guilt and shame and allow the warriors within to claim their seat. Love the Crow and grow.

Journaling Invitations

How has who I am shaped the ways I lead others and myself?

————

Which of my unconscious patterns might
be showing up in my organization?

————

How have those patterns benefited my organization?

————

How might they be holding it back?

————

CHAPTER 8

Heartbreak, Resilience, and the Path to Equanimity

THE HEARTBREAK OF EVERY DAY

Here's a fact to break your heart: chestnut trees, parents, children, friends, lovers, and dreams all die.

Our children—stepping into our footprints—struggle, fumbling their way through to adulthood, bearing skinned and scarred knees, broken hearts, and the imprint of wretched disappointment. They manage this while navigating the unrelenting compulsion to find the person they were born to be, toiling against forces that would have them be someone else. The resulting heartbreak becomes the means of self-discovery and, ultimately, self-creation.

A CEO develops a rare blood cancer and funding for the company is threatened. A fiancé calls off the wedding a month before the ceremony. A marriage ends when a spouse dies. Customers reject us. Investors abandon us. Our companies, the embodiments of our wishes and dreams, crash and burn after years of riding the roller coaster. Our ability to love and be loved, to feel safe and that we belong is challenged daily by the everyday-ness of heartbreak and struggle.

We struggle with these painful realities—of birth, old age, sickness, and death—trying desperately, usually vainly, to see the heartbreak of every day not as evidence of our own unworthiness and unlovability but as life merely unfolding, as intended. That struggle exacerbates the everyday pain; we struggle to accept the roller-coaster ride for what it is: *life*.

We compound that pain by misunderstanding the notion of resiliency—the capacity to bounce back. So often we're told that we should be resilient, but we're rarely handed a map to get there. Worse, we mistakenly believe that arriving at that state is the point of it all. The point of riding the roller coaster isn't to be better at riding roller coasters; it's to learn how not to board the roller coaster at all. Coney Island's Cyclone is best appreciated from the ground. Resiliency isn't the goal; it's the path. The goal is the equanimity of a warrior.

The first step on the path of resiliency and the movement toward a warrior's equanimity are taken by having your heart broken open by the everyday skinning of your child's knee, the dismembering of a tree, or the death of a spouse.

FAILURE AND THE PASSAGE OF TREES

I find impermanence to be the most heartrending attribute of the passage of time.

As a boy, the horse chestnut tree provided the safety of a

hollow in which I could temporarily escape the shame of our poverty and the angry, confusing yelling that would often enough lead to violence. As a boy, I found love deep within the fall-dropped spiky chestnut, which remained milky white and soft and cool to the touch. I found safety when that milky-white softness would emerge after weeks buried deep in my sock drawer, with the shimmering sienna of a blood bay Arabian. As a boy, I found belonging beneath the spreading five-fingered leaves of the tree as my best friend, Marcus, and I tossed a football high into the branches, hoping to knock down clusters of the spiky-skinned nuts.

And then came the day when I'd heard the beep-beep-beep of the yellow-orange New York City Parks Department pay-loader as it backed up to scoop up another load of the newly cut, sawdusty logs that were once, in total, the chestnut tree, now felled. My sanctuary gone. Beep-beep-beep.

"It's gone, it's gone, it's gone," I'd wept into my mother's apron, her hand stroking my head, smoothing the muscles of my neck. The heartfelt "there, there" of my mother's comforting drawing me into the knowledge that, through it all, here, in that place of heartache, confusion, and fear, was the love of home. Here one minute, gone the next, heartbreak leading to comfort.

I'm haunted by the smell of freshly cut wood.

Polar explorer Ben Saunders first contacted me in 2008. I was still finding my footing as a coach, and he needed someone to help him figure out how to finance his passion, the work he was born to do. Or so he told me.

"I was only a few days out," he began, "when the ski binding broke and I had to call the whole thing off." A few months earlier, he'd set out to establish a new record—the fastest to ski to the North Pole and back, from the Canadian approach. A few days in, the entire enterprise had failed. And here he was, broke, with no means of support. His entrepreneurial endeavor had run out of cash and a friend had said I might help him figure out how to raise money to keep the effort alive.

I startled him by noting that it must have sucked to have had to call it off. He laughed with relief. It was nice to hear someone say, simply, "Well, that sucked." But then, as I recall, he started to cry—which, I know now, was not what he expected when he'd called the entrepreneur's coach.

"Do I even have a superpower?" Kent Cavender-Bares asked me when we recorded our conversation for a podcast. His wife, having heard another episode, had encouraged him to listen and, then, reach out to talk. His question in response to my exploration of how those things we've tossed into our shadow have a deep power that, when accessed with compassion and skill, can drive our creativity. He cried quietly when I noted that his struggle must be so painful.

Behind his question lay the heartbreak that comes from having struggled so mightily to launch a business—in this case a robot designed to help farmers apply fertilizer and pesticides more efficient and less harmful to the land they caretake. Kent's dream is to heal the land while enabling people to grow more food. The heartbreak evident in his implicit questions: "What if my deep integrity, my commitment to simply telling how it is, is the reason we're unable to fund-raise? Do I even have a superpower?" Would the company be better off with someone else as CEO? Would my family and the world be better off if I stopped trying so hard to be an entrepreneur and just went back to the world of work, where we are seen merely as Tab A headed for Slot B?

THIS RIDE IS DARK AND SCARY

While heartbreak is the early step on the path to equanimity, fear is the stumbling block leading to the sin of inaction. Fearing the dark rides of the Coney Island of the mind, we choose not to act. Fearing Paris, we stay close to home. Fearing broken skis, failed businesses, and the scars that come from skinned knees, we stay small—listening more to our Loyal Soldier's fear-filled and protective whispered warnings than to the quickening thump-thump, thump-thump, thump-thump of a heart that knows how it's meant to be.

Fear, and not some lack of grit or resiliency, blocks the emergence of our fully actualized and equanimous self. The warrior crouches behind walls of fear. Life should come with a placard: WARNING! THIS RIDE IS DARK AND SCARY.

What is it we fear? Well, first, the threats to love, safety, and belonging. But, really, we fear death, the pain of freshly cut logs from the felled sanctuary hurts. We fear shame because it rends our sense of who we might be and—we believe—threatens our worthiness to be loved. We fear love because the object of our love may jump ship and abandon us, leaving us as bereft as a ten-year-old boy amid the cut logs of a sanctuary tree.

We fear the change inherent in our children growing into adulthood, the death of those close to us, the end of decades-long relationships. My fear of impermanence leads me to wish to hold even the bittersweet painful moments of life in amber, preserved like a prehistoric insect, to be admired but, ironically, no longer lived.

This morning as I slipped on my sneakers, I was overwhelmed by a memory of shopping with my daughter, Emma. She must have been five. She needed new sneakers and, being the efficient shopper that I am, I snatched her up and took her to the local mall. I waited—patiently, I told myself—for her to choose which of the hundreds of pairs her five-year-old heart would like.

The chosen pair fitted, I paid at the register, and with her tiny hand in mine, we walked briskly from the store.

"Daddy," she asked, slightly out of breath as her little legs strode to keep pace with my much larger, more important daddy-legs, "Daddy, did you ever buy something, and . . ." she paused, caught her breath, and continued, "and realize after you've left the store that you really wanted the other thing?"

Screech! Stop! I looked down to see fearful tears running down her cheeks. In my bid to be an efficient, effective father, I had failed to be with her and feel her heart. I bent, picking her up in one motion, and apologized for moving so quickly in the world that I did not notice my little girl's heart.

I want to hold forever the bitterness of my having forgotten her and the sweetness of my having been called to take my seat as a warrior dad. I want to remember forever that we marched back to that store and bought a second pair because, in the end, it didn't matter that, having worn the shoes outside the store, we couldn't return those wrong shoes. The warrior dad bought the right shoes, the shoes his daughter wanted, and was reminded of the importance of listening to his little girl's heart.

I want to be haunted by that bittersweet feeling forever; out of such heartbreak grew the resiliency with which I learned to listen to the fearful hearts of those I love and ride through the heartbreak of every day.

THE LOVINGKINDNESS OF TRUE GRIT

I often speak of resiliency, and no matter how much I try to do otherwise, I still manage to come across as if I'm speaking about grit. So, I'll speak of grit. True grit is more than the capacity to grin and bear it. To understand true grit, we need to understand false grit.

False grit is brittle. It's the sense that we are nothing if we can't take a punch. In fact, we define "taking a punch" as the ability to not feel pain when we are punched. False grit is dangerous. It feeds a stubbornness that, in turn, can feed delusion. We mistake the tendency to delude ourselves that our relationship will improve, our companies will succeed, if only we double down on our old patterns, grip the steering wheel until our knuckles whiten, and bear down. Stubbornness is not the hallmark of the warrior.

Leaders who persist out of stubbornness, believing themselves to be gritty, are at best delusional and, at worst, reckless.

False grit awakens the Crow. One of its implicit messages is that we should persist to prove that we aren't as unworthy as the Crow claims. Yet a second implicit message is that if we feel like shit after being punched in the face, it must mean that we *are* shit. The only way to escape the grip of false grit is to recognize its falsity.

True grit is kind. True grit is persistent. True grit persists not in holding on to false beliefs against all evidence but in believing in one's inherent lovability and worthiness. True grit is the leader believing in the team's purpose, its capacity to overcome obstacles, and the relevancy of the cause. True grit acknowledges the potential of failure, embraces the fear of disappointment, and rallies the team to reach and try, regardless of the potential of loss.

True grit, the capacity to stick with something to the end, stems from knowing oneself well enough to be able to forgive oneself. To have inquired deeply and steadily enough to find the deep sense of purpose that is beyond a personal mission statement. In that knowing of oneself, one is then able to stand as a single warrior amid a community of brokenhearted fellow leaders.

We see true grit in the lovingkindness of compassionate leaders, those who embody the Buddhist principle of bodhicitta and strive to be of service to others. I feel the truth of that and yet I battle my own obstacles: How do you serve others when your heart is pained and your warrior is terrified?

SITTING WITH SUFFERING

I sat still in a stuffy white tent, despite the nearly unbearable August heat in the mountains of Colorado. Six years after my first encounter with Pema Chödrön, I took in her teachings again. Late-afternoon thunderstorms rolled in the distance, promising cool relief. We were three hundred students in all; many sobbed gently while they watched their breath and eased their monkey-minds.

At the talk that followed the sitting, I'd made my way to the microphone to ask a question. "Ani Pema," I asked, my voice breaking slightly as I used her honorific title. "How do I forgive those who hurt me so badly? How do I free myself from the haunting pain of my childhood?" Shading her eyes to see the questioner more clearly, she smiled and said, "Oh, hello, Jerry."

She then recounted the story of the woman who, having suffered the unbearable heartbreak of the death of her child, was asked by the Buddha to go to every household of those who had not suffered heartbreak and collect a mustard seed. "Of course," she smiled gently, "the woman came back to the Buddha empty-handed."

The point wasn't for me to make small my suffering by comparing myself to others. The point was to lean into the universality of the suffering. "I'd like you to add a practice to your meditation," she answered. "Please consider all the children—yourself included—from the past, present, and future who have, are, and will suffer equally. Send them love."

I began doing that, opening my heart to exactly that searing, piercing pain—the universal pain of children who do not feel loved, safe, or that they belong—and I sat still with all our suffering.

Years later, I astonished myself by concluding that, in the wake of an earthquake in an area called Yushu in the ethnically Tibetan region of China, I would do what I could to alleviate suffering. I was astonished by the impulse; I'd never done anything like that before.

I rode into the devastated city five months after the quake. Buildings everywhere lay toppled, and amid the piles of rubble that had been homes, clinics, and schools, the streets were barely discernible.

"At least there aren't bodies in the streets anymore," said one of my guides, a woman who'd been in Yushu shortly after the quake. We then spent our days handing out thick, cotton tents, blankets, and other supplies. We wandered through the rubble trying to help as we could. We came across a man caring for a deaf and mute nun, the stench of her incontinence overwhelming. He'd lost his wife the morning of the earthquake. The stupa, the sacred hemispherical structure containing relics around which she'd been making her ritualistic circumambulation, had toppled with the quake, killing her.

He wept in gratitude for the food, clothing, and blankets we left. Putting his hands together, he spoke a rapid Tibetan. One of my friends, Sonam, another Tibetan guide, began crying as he spoke with the man. Assuming he was giving us thanks, I asked Sonam what he'd said. "He was praying that, if an earthquake should happen again, and if a life needs to be taken, it should be him for he'd never want another person to feel the heartbreak that he now feels."

Heartbreak is universal. Keeping one's heart open to the suffering of others, even upon the failure of our companies and the death of a tree, is rare and the truest grit of all.

True grit is an expression of resiliency. True grit is not only having your heart broken open by the death of a chestnut tree, the killing fall of a stupa's stonework, and the swoon of a roller-coaster drop, but it's also managing to keep that heart open despite those losses. Bodhicitta means "awakened mind," but it connotes open heart. Your mind cannot awaken while your heart remains closed.

When leaders allow their hearts to stay broken open, they're able to recognize that the suffering they encounter every day among their employees, colleagues, and investors is universal. Their fear of failure, for example, is the very same fear their investors carry. It may be distorted by the fun-house effect of the investors' structural power—distorted by the investors' Loyal Soldier and other shadowed qualities into an aggression—but it is nevertheless the same fear. All loss threatens the love, safety, and belonging of even those who hold power.

During your next board meeting, collect a mustard seed from all those present who don't worry that the company's failure will threaten their love, safety, and sense of belonging. During your next all-hands staff meeting, collect mustard seeds from all those who haven't feared the loss of their job, disappointing their loved ones, having their Crow's exhortations about their impostor status proved correct, or otherwise tumbling backward down the staircase of life. Attempt to collect those mustard seeds and then stare at your empty hands.

As leaders, our task is to feel our way through the heartbreaking, fear-inducing roller-coaster rides, learning not to vomit with each rise and dip. Then, just as we've built up the resiliency needed to recover from each nauseating dip, we find that we no longer have the need for it. The little train that makes up the Cyclone comes to a stop and we finally, wisely, get off the ride.

LISTENING FOR EQUANIMITY

My sister Nicki has tacked up above her desk at work a quote I once gave to a reporter. She tells me it makes her proud of me. I'd said that equanimity boils down to this: "Everything's great, and I'm okay. Everything sucks, and I'm okay. Through years of radically inquiring within my broken-open heart, sitting still with that pain and its universal nature, I've been able to experience the occasional true equanimity."

Sitting still, listening to the Earth, I learned the power of contented simplicity. Ten years ago, I made one of my teachers laugh out loud when I told him of my plans to go on a vision quest. Having migrated from China as a boy, he spent most of his fifty years in the United States. Having been born in China, he'd still occasionally use the "you Americans" construction.

"You Americans," he said with a shake of his head, "You think you can schedule a vision." Laughing, he asked, "Do you think insight is going to coincide with your vacation?"

His doubts notwithstanding, I left my home on Long Island and traveled to the four corners where Nevada, Colorado, Utah, and Arizona meet. My own doubts notwithstanding, I traveled to sit in a kiva with guides who—I did not know at the time—would become my lifelong friends. My own fears notwithstanding, I found myself asking permission from a twisted and gnarled pine, before tying up my shelter, to use its branches for support. My self-consciousness notwithstanding, I found myself hearing a new name for myself as the wind bent and shook the tops of the pines all around me.

During my solo time, a time of fasting and solitude, I connected to the love, safety, and belonging that came not from those around me but from my own self. "Oh, so this is who I am," I said, astonished by my discovery. "Oh, this, this is my pain." Sheltered by only a thin yellow sheet of nylon, naked except for light khaki shorts, taking small sips of water so as not to die in the desert, with no books, no journal, no other means of distraction from the essence of me, I sat still, my skin raw and exposed, my senses widening with an animal ferocity. I heard everything. I felt the Earth's passage through space and, therefore, time. I heard the wisdom of boulders older than humans. I walked among shards of busted pottery older than the United States. I heard stories told by a people who railed against the impermanence of their lives by leaping desert chasms to leave handprints on canyon walls.

Hearing all that, I dug deep into the sandbank of the river from which I drew my water. I lit a fire and praised those who'd guided me to this point in my life. Under the gaze of millennia-old boulders, I vomited the heartbreak and pain of my childhood wounds until my throat was raw, my cheeks burned by tears, and my stomach, pained and emptied, had nothing to offer.

I had no need beyond a thin sheet of nylon, a few sips of water, and knowledge that the Earth was able to hold and witness all that I have been, all that I am, and all that I will become. I sat in that contented simplicity as Grandfather Boulder lovingly held it all, receiving it as if to say, "Even with all this, you are still my son. You are loved, you are safe, and you belong to me as surely as your brothers and sisters, the boulders."

The Earth held me, and I then learned the equanimity that comes from listening. I returned the favor with a poem of my own:

Listen

On a brightening morning
When dark places seem furthest,
Brother Warrior comes,
Helping me remember me.
He stands with legs firmly rooted
in the earth,
arms at his side,
palms open,
back strong,
heart exposed.
"You were not given this life to carry only your sorrow.
You were not given this life only to lament.
Make holy that which you were given:
Go and listen."
Over his shoulder
Grandfather Boulder,
With his never-ending smile,
Looks on his two sons of the Earth:
"Listening," he reminds, "opens that which pain has closed.
In listening we are healing.
We are never healed but forever healing.
We are never loved but forever loving."

Our hearts close and we become both the builders and wardens of our prisons, our mind-forged manacles rattling with shame and fearful cries of our unlovability. Listening, he taught me, breaks the chains. Listening to others, Ani Pema taught me, snaps the bonds of our woeful lamentations. Listening to ourselves, deep self-inquiry, turns resiliency into growth and equanimity.

My rightful, appropriate, healthy response to the wounds of childhood was anger. Unmet, disregarded, the anger turned into rage. Lacking the skills to work with the anger and rage, it would manifest into an anxious doubt about my safety, my belonging. Yet, despite that ju-jitsu move of anger into anxiety, my underlying rage remained. Hulk remained.

Following the Grandfather Boulder's instructions to listen to my own self, I began to inquire after my rage, to look at the fears and the pain that lay behind it. I visualized that rage as the sweating, red-faced boy whose only way of surviving was to try to chase with fury those who would humiliate him. Assuring that boy that he had a right to his anger, I then asked about the ways he'd been denied and banished. I asked after the hurt behind the rage and sat still with the stories he shared.

Slowly, slowly and working together, we reassigned the rage. The red-faced little boy no longer needed to chase and smash to guard against shame. That fierce rage stopped being a dangerous enemy and became a fierce guardian of the scared and less powerful. The red-faced boy transformed into the guardian of my tender, open heart.

I listened to myself; I grew.

JUST AS I AM, I AM ENOUGH

At our boot camps, the simple power of a walk with a friend often comes across like magic. With a few simple instructions such as "listen and don't fix," folks come back from a twenty-minute stroll, weeping, having experienced the power of listening and of being heard. Or having the burden of a secret held to keep others safe lifted and shared, making the load just a little lighter.

We gathered in a circle to reflect on what had happened and to tell each other's stories. When Alisha heard her partner say the word *burden* once, twice, and finally three times, she began crying. "I never knew I carried that word, *burden*, so deeply."

She then shared a story of growing up in a family that felt like a burden on the whole town. Beloved, they depended on the kindness of strangers. And rather than enhancing the sense of belonging that came from community, it manacled Alisha with the shame of poverty. When her pillar-of-the-community father left the family (no doubt in pursuit of his own love, safety, and belonging), she took on the burden of caring for her mother and brother. Yet another hallmark of the entrepreneur; yet another instance of premature promotion into adulthood.

She built a company on the foundations of a business she'd launched in her teens. One designed to generate a profit, no matter how small, from day one. And, furthermore, one never in need of capital—never a burden to others. But this complex of "never be a burden and always relieve others' burdens" became a prison, and behind those bars, her resentment grew.

On her walk, she shared things about herself that she wished the people in her life knew about her. As her partner listened, she was able to hear her story, and the rattling of her manacles. She heard the fear, shame, and pain behind her resentful anger toward her brother. Later she went for a walk with her mother and brother. They listened to each other.

The healing that followed the listening became a retelling and reimagining of the narrative of heartbreak that dominated their childhood of poverty and abandonment, confusion and shame. The listening led to a healing that moved them past the resiliency of "we'll never be a burden to others" into the equanimity of the acceptance of the pain while dropping the shackles of the story of the pain. The stories they told about their experience were transformed from instruments of survival into no-longer-needed artifacts in an otherwise equanimous life.

Learning to listen, as I have done, helped me inquire into my own ways, to see my ghosts and programmed ways of being. Listening with an open, non-judging heart allowed me to learn when I'd had enough of the world and its harsh need to change me into someone I am not.

That learned declaration of *enough* supports the grittiest, most equanimous expression possible: that as broken-open as I may be, I am enough. Just as I am, I am *enough*.

THE SPACE BETWEEN CLOUDS AND WAVES

"The space between what's wrong and right is where you'll find me hiding," sings Dave Matthews. The space between is where I am and the me that's hiding there is enough.

One of the most striking images from my many trips to Tibet was the reverently preserved dried skulls of great teachers. Occasionally, usually in the homes of a village elder, you'll see among treasured items, the top half of such a skull. Moving beyond the impulse to recoil at such objects, I'm always drawn in by the firmly held belief that amid the scribbles of what must have been bone meeting brain are auspicious imprints testifying to the holiness of the departed. It's believed that the scribbly indentations on the underside of the skulls of great teachers often form the shape of a sitting Buddha. Buddhists believe so fervently in the power of equanimity, the fundamental basic goodness of all beings, the fundamental Buddha-nature of all things, that they see the Buddha in stones, trees, skies, and the bones of long-dead teachers. Buddha-nature resides in the most unexpected places.

In my struggle to fully take in the fundamental goodness of all things, myself included, I strained to see what was so clear to my host in his delicate relic. Even now, his wishing to believe, as well as his wish to be believed, is seared into my consciousness, fixed in place by the sensuous smell of burning dried yak dung. For me, such is Tibet.

It was in Tibet that I first tasted the equanimity that arises from wishing that the pain of death, loss, and failure were mine to bear, easing the lived experiences of those around me. From my time in Tibet, I came to understand what clouds and waves can teach us about facing suffering with true grit.

Of all the Buddhist saints I've come to know, only Milarepa seems like someone who could have been raised in Brooklyn. It's not merely his "Eat me if you wish" attitude in the face of monstrous demons that makes me feel like he could have walked down Flatbush Avenue. It's the story of his heartbreak turned into resilience and equanimity. His father died when he was just a boy, and his life of wealth, comfort, and ease were turned upside down. Promoted prematurely, he took on the burden of caring for his now-bereft family. In her heartbreak, his mother encouraged him to take up black magic. His leadership skills were honed at the whetstone of his mother's suffering and anger.

He traveled the area robbing and murdering. It's said that he wore the fingerbones of his murder victims as a necklace. Later, he met the great teacher Marpa, who, through a series of backbreaking (and ego-demolishing) tasks, helped Milarepa become a saintly poet and beloved meditation master.

In one of the many songs that define his teachings, a student asks the master, "I can contemplate the sky, but clouds make me uneasy. Milarepa, tell me how to meditate on clouds." Tell me, in effect, how I can achieve equanimity when the clouds get in the way of my seeing the empty, immense sky.

The student goes on and asks again about the difficulty he has in meditating on the calm beauty and serenity of the sea when all he can see is the waves.

Wise Milarepa, the young boy who turned his suffering into violence only to learn how to truly be with his pain, answers, "If the sky's as easy as you say, clouds are just the sky's play." He then adds that "waves are just the sea's play." We can't separate the clouds from sky or the waves from the sea. There is no space between our thoughts, however painful they might be, and our mind. "Let your mind stay within the sea," he advises, and so, too, "Let your mind stay within your mind."

THIS TOO SHALL PASS

Whether the heartbreak of daily life leads to resiliency and equanimity is then a function of seeing the clouds, the waves, and thoughts at play. Every rise and fall of the roller coaster is life at play.

What, then, is equanimity? It's the space between right and wrong, guilt and innocence, sad and happy, greedy and satiated.

It's the space between wishing things were different from what they are and bitterly giving up and giving in to the fuck-my-life-ness of the world and its harsh pain of birth, old age, sickness, and death. It's the space where, dissatisfied with life as it is, we strive forward, despite knowing that our efforts may fail, will likely fail. We build our companies, our castles in the sky, our mandala sand paintings knowing that the winds will inevitably shift, and all will be gone. It's the space where, despite the death of a tree, we can feel the glorious reassurance that all shall be well.

For me, equanimity feels like coming home to a house I once occupied before I lost the ability to see the waves, the clouds, and my thoughts at play.

In the ten years I've known Ben Saunders, I've never once asked him why he does the whole polar thing. Part of the reason I didn't ask was that I always thought that doing so would annoy him. But another reason why I didn't ask was that I knew he was out on the ice looking for something. I was just never entirely sure what it was he was looking for.

In his attempt to complete his friend Henry's journey, the solo crossing of Antarctica, it became clear to me what it was he was looking for. As I've written, about midway through the first leg of the journey, Ben was struggling with the formidable sastrugi, the wind-driven ridges on the surface of rock-hard snow. His progress was slow, and it was becoming apparent that, unless he cut his rations in half, he'd run out of food before he could be resupplied. He was faced with either stopping short of his goal, a failure from a false grit point of view, or plunging on, risking his life and dying as his friend Henry had done.

During our satellite phone call, when I'd given him the Zen-like advice to take only small steps, I struggled to understand my role: Was I supposed to encourage him to soldier on or was I to tell him to call it quits? Soon enough I dropped my own notions of fixing the situation and simply listened. As we talked, I heard something different in his voice. Yes, as he often did when we spoke while he was on the ice, he complained about how challenging things were. He was hungry. He was tired. He was cold. But this time I noticed a calmness in his voice, and when we spoke about his stopping the trip early, he said something remarkable. "Jerry," he said, speaking of his then fiancée and now wife, Philippa ("Pip"), "I've now got someone to come home to."

I realized then what it was that kept him going to the ice: he'd been looking for home.

All humans seek love, safety, and belonging. For years, I thought Ben wandered the cold deserts because he was looking for love, safety, and belonging. Through his struggle with the sastrugi, with the potential heartbreak of failing to live up to his heroic challenge of finishing his friend and mentor

Henry's dream, Ben came to the resiliency of carrying on and the true grit of stopping the journey when continuing would have been madness. With Pip in mind, he found the way to the love, safety, belonging, and equanimity of home.

I remember lying on Dr. Sayres's couch, speaking of the hole in my chest that never seemed to close, and I shared the memory of my Howdy Doody puppet. Howdy Doody, the two-foot-long plug for that hole in my chest. Each night I hugged him tightly, wishing he'd enter me, filling that space inside, that deep emptiness that seemed forever a part of me.

"What did he feel like?" she asked me.

"Mine. Me. I don't know . . . like a piece of me, the missing piece of me."

Mom, uncomfortable that her son was so attached to a doll, shamed me for loving him and, in that shame, I secreted him away in a closet. Boys don't cry. Boys don't play with dolls. Boys don't have holes in their hearts.

"How did it feel when he was gone?" she asked.

"Empty. I was bereft."

"Like when the horse chestnut tree was cut down?" she offered gently, understanding me in a way few have ever.

"Exactly." Without the tree, without my friend, I was bereft, homeless, unsheltered, and ill prepared to face the world.

"Did I even deserve to feel at home?" I asked through tear-filled doubts. Did I even deserve equanimity?

She quieted my fears and yet again shared with me wisdom from her own life experience. "Oh, Jerry," she said with that so comforting chiding of a loving and understanding parent. "Don't you know that this too shall pass? *Gam zeh ya'avor?*"

She'd shared that phrase, "This too shall pass," for years. I'd walk into her office, high from the glorious achievements of my hard-fought life. She'd laugh and tell me she was proud of me and then lovingly remind me that this too shall pass.

Just as frequently, she'd offer the same wisdom when the heartbreaks of the past and present would threaten to overwhelm me: "Oh, Jerry, don't you know that this too shall pass?"

She was right, of course. I learned to use each heartbreak—be it the memory of feeling bereft and ripped open by heartache or a present experience of being overwhelmed by disappointment and grief—as a reminder of that wisdom.

The hole in my chest—the space between wishing for a world that could be and seeing the world as it is—was filled by the blessing of equanimity and the gravity of life at times when I was felled by the deaths of loved ones, dreams, and trees, but also enlightened and lifted by grace. Met by true grit, my heartbreak gave way to true belonging, true peace of mind, and truly coming home.

Journaling Invitations

How has my heart been broken?

————

What have I learned about myself as a
result of that heart being broken?

————

In what ways do I embody resiliency?

————

What does a life of peace and equanimity feel like?

CHAPTER 9

————

Leadership and the Art of Growing Up

For Parker

L ilac, honeysuckle, and diesel fumes perfumed the air as a stream of cars thumped across the expansion joints of the Brooklyn Bridge. On that late-spring night, Chad Dickerson and I shared tears and beer while considering not only the course of our lives but especially the twists of the most recent weeks.

What had led Chad to be fired from his role as CEO at Etsy? What had he done wrong? Had he been the CEO we both thought he was?

I struggled with my own doubts. Had I, his coach and con-sigliere, failed him? Had each of us, in our own way, simply not been good enough? We sat beside each other on the top of the picnic table, shoulders nearly touching, allowing our broken-open hearts to lead us both to a place of inquiry and warriorship.

We took in the possibility of each of our failures. We con-sidered all that we'd done right and all that we'd regretted. And—our backs unbent—we clinked bottles and toasted, acknowledging how much we'd each grown. We knew that Chad, in announcing his departure and leaving the team he'd led for six years, would have to bring forth the dignity and grace that lay within his body since his North Carolina boyhood. The grace and dignity of a man toiling at a proj-ect not because it might bring wealth or approbation but be-cause it was his job to do it. Standing next to him, I glimpsed the strength of his father, who led road repair gangs, making the highways safe for North Carolinians to drive to work, to school, to church, to the store for a loaf of bread. Good work, done well, for the right reasons.

As I think back—under those bright stars—it wasn't just Chad's warrior that emerged. I, too, was transformed. I, too, had to reach deep inside to find and take my seat.

That late-spring night, two men sat on a picnic table on a Brooklyn rooftop as cars and trucks pounded out a ceaseless rhythm. Two men sat on a rooftop and rediscovered the true leaders, the true warriors, the true adults waiting to come forth. As the lilac-honeysuckle-diesel-perfumed air filled their lungs, it mixed with a hint of the sticky-sweet smell of sour lemon drops, and the two men used those stars to chart a way ahead.

While Chad began to find his post-CEO way that night, I, too, rediscovered the warrior within. A decade ago, in a desert in Utah, Grandfather Boulder instructed me to listen and, in so doing, open that which pain had closed. I cut short my wondering if his pain was my failing. I let go of that fear, knowing this scene wasn't about me. I saw clearly that my job had never been to save, to fix, or to prevent my friend from failing. My job remained what it had always been: to listen, to bear witness, and, in doing so, to midwife the birth of the warrior.

My work isn't to save anyone from the heartbreak of everyday—not my clients, not my children, not my friends, not my loves. If I were I to manage to pull it off, I would end up standing in the way of their finding equanimity. My work is to bear witness to the growth of those whom I love and care for. My work is to stand shoulder to shoulder, as when two men sat on a rooftop and found their way to the love, safety, belonging, and equanimity of brokenhearted warriors.

Taking your seat; allowing your heart to break and stay open; accepting all the ways you strive to feel love, safety, and belonging allow you to let go of the striving and welcome in equanimity.

STRIVING NO MORE

The angle of the late-afternoon Colorado sun intensified both its light and heat. I moved to lower the shade, cutting the glare and the burn. My friend Brad Feld and I sat on his back porch while his golden retrievers vied for our affection. We spoke of big and small things. We reminisced. We recalled stories from two decades of friendship. We caught up on recent stories, present-day stories, of lives unfolding, hearts breaking, and the gravity that comes from becoming more and more ourselves.

"I'm working harder than I'd like," he tells me as we both nod, recognizing the tendency in each of us to do that. We know that neither of us will ever really stop working; for us, working means thinking, talking, connecting, and creating. "The difference now," he says, referring to his fifty-something self, "the difference from earlier in my life is simple: I'm no longer striving."

Seat taken, he no longer needs to define himself by what he's doing. Seat taken, he can allow the sadness of everyday heartbreak—his and that of those he loves—to wash over and through him. Seat taken, the gentle, openhearted warrior emerges, and we laugh and speak of our approaching elderhood.

Taking your seat leads to equanimity. Taking your seat means defining your life. Acknowledging that which you've come to regret while seeing the possibilities in all that's before you. Seat taken, you get to define your leadership and your life. Or, I suppose, your life in this moment, for the process of becoming doesn't ever end. It's always unfolding. Life is growth and change, and while the impermanence of time passing is heartbreaking, it creates the ground from which the new me, the warrior in me, emerges. This is life unfolding as intended. This is becoming the warrior adult. This is the gift of leadership. This is the art of growing up.

THE GIFTS OF LEADERSHIP

So much of what I've learned about growing up came from learning to lead.

In fact, the process of becoming *me* made me a better leader. The two processes, becoming a leader and becoming ourselves, are intertwined and interdependent; better leaders are better humans and better humans are better leaders. Leadership lessons, then, are, at their core, lessons in humanity.

Sometimes the belief systems that are most difficult to overcome aren't the ghosts in the machine of our childhood. Sometimes the most difficult belief systems fall under the rubric of "conventional wisdom." Conventional wisdom, for example, dictates that, in our process of becoming warrior-leaders, we focus on the hard things. Big rocks, folks say knowingly. "Break down the big rocks and then focus on the little rocks." But how do you discern a big rock from a little rock?

Moreover, when we're in that hair-on-fire state, and the Crow is cawing relentlessly about the risks of failure, even the easy things become hard. Conventional wisdom doesn't tell us that when you care so much, when the risk of heartbreak is so high, when the potential loss of respect and self-esteem and the risk of humiliation and attendant shame from your bitter and sure defeat by life are so great, it's *all* big rocks and it's *all* hard. But with discernment, with radically inquiring within, we can separate the hard and complicated from the hard and simple. In fact, forget focusing on the easy or hard; learn to distinguish between the complicated and the simple.

Running a business, for example, is simple. As my grandfather would say, just make sure you have more money at the end of the day than you did at the beginning of the day. Make sure you have enough money, so your grandson can always find safety and love in a canister of lemon drops. Simple but hard.

What makes hard things like running a business complicated is leaders' avoiding doing their work. When we don't do our work, we stand in the way of our own growth. When we fail to grow, we hold back others, and we warp and twist the organizations we seek to serve. We turn the work of others into the work of covering up our failings, plugging the holes in our chests, and living out the commands of the ghosts in our machines. What makes all of life complicated, and not just hard, is this unwillingness to do the work that's ours to do; our unwillingness to live the examined life.

When leaders fail to look at themselves, they turn their inner turmoil and very human contradictions outward. Further, unable to face their fears, they mask the anxiety with aggression. As my friend and mentor Parker Palmer, teaches, "Violence is what we do when we don't know what to do with our suffering." Violence to our planet, violence to our communities, and violence to ourselves are what we do when we refuse to look inward and work with the heartbreak of the everyday.

Some of us seek to create havens to shelter ourselves from the rigor of this work. We'll give ourselves over to an existential materialism, seeking refuge not in the rigor of the truth of life as it is but in spiritual and psychological delusion. Such havens are spawned when we convince ourselves that we're done with inner exploration or we assure ourselves that the organizations we've created are havens of love, safety, and belonging, never checking back, though, for fear that we're wrong.

We need to be vigilant and rigorous in cutting through our delusions. Such havens, warned James Baldwin, are "high-priced." They can demand of us that we live the unexamined, delusional life. "I still believe that the unexamined life is not worth living: and I know that self-delusion," wrote Baldwin, "in service of no matter what small or lofty cause, is a price no writer can afford." No writer, I'll add, no leader, and, finally, no adult. Paraphrasing Baldwin, I'd say that a leader's subject is himself and the world and "it requires every ounce of stamina he can summon to attempt to look on himself and the world as they are."

Seeing ourselves and the world as they are is a cornerstone of good leadership and the well-lived adulthood. One of the most startling challenges I will put to a client comes from my bastardization of a Zen aphorism: This being so, so what? Things being as they are, what will you do about it?

Avoiding havens of self-delusion, maturing with a fierce regard for the truth of who and how we are, allows us the grace and freedom to live with contradictory, confusing, and ambivalent feelings. Dr. Sayres taught me that one of the hallmarks of mental health is the ability to hold conflicting feelings. Acknowledging that we hold those contradictions, accepting that we can both love and hate precisely the same things, is core to accepting ourselves all the way down to our bones.

Contradiction and ambivalence, then, are not further evidence of our failings. We so fear being labeled hypocrites that we cast about for masks, lest people see our ambivalence as weakness. Just as we, as adult humans, can both love and hate, we, as human leaders, can be both terrified and excited by the future.

The leader fears failure and yet believes in the team's potential to succeed. Parents fret over their childen's skinned knees and broken hearts but celebrate their separation and individuation. Partners allow the space for both love and fear in the relationship, trusting that the irrational messiness of their vulnerable and real selves will be wholly, unfailingly, and lovingly accepted. In doing so, in accepting that within themselves, they create a true haven whereby their person, their Other, can be wholly, fully, their messy selves trusting that they, too, will be lovingly accepted. Stepping out of such havens, we are called upon to be loved, to be made safe, and to know that we belong not despite our failings but with compassionate regard for the gifts of our imperfections.

Leading and living in this unsheltered way invite us to take our seats as the most caring, most calm voice in the room—in our relationships, our families, our companies, and our communities.

My co-founder, Ali Schultz, taught me the wisdom of horses. Horses, with their supernatural ability to use their limbic nervous systems to discern truth and congruency, do not base their choice of the leader of their herd on strength or intellectual wisdom. Nor is their choice based on which member might keep the herd safe from a predator wolf. They choose the one who feels the group best and who cares the most. They choose the horse—usually a mare—who is most capable of holding that care in a way that calms the whole group. They're marked by the attunement to the inner and outer needs of those they have the honor to serve and lead.

When leaders allow themselves the grace of being fierce

with the reality of their messy broken-open hearts—the truth of life as it is and not as they wish it to be—the individuals in the group are offered the opportunity, as are our loved ones, to let go of their fears of failing or disappointing and focus on the business at hand; the worthiness of the shared task as well as the personal tasks of growing up and into their fullest potential as humans.

This being fierce with the reality of what is requires the bravery to ask of oneself three challenging and yet powerfully liberating questions:

- What am I not saying that needs to be said?

- What am I saying (in words or deeds) that's not being heard?

- What's being said that I'm not hearing?

Dr. Sayres taught me those questions to release me from the grip of my psychosomatic migraines. In doing so, she gave me—and all those with whom I've now worked—the gift of *prajna*.

My New York office is decorated with soothing blues and photographs taken from the various wondrous places I've visited. My main chair, the seat I take when I'm coaching, is placed opposite a couch and under a photo from game one of the 2000 World Series (when my beloved Yankees defeated the Mets). Most clients will sit on the couch and I can emotionally hold them while we do the work. Out of their sight, and well within my view, is a statue of Manjushri, one of the oldest of the many Buddhist bodhisattvas. My golden Manjushri wields a flaming sword, representing the transcendent wisdom that cuts down ignorance, duality, and delusion.

What am I not saying? What's really going on? What confusing and contradictory emotions are blocking our insight and wisdom to know the way forward? The leader best able to cut through the miasma of confused and conflicting emotions, to answer such questions and see the nature of the reality of the organization's triumphs and struggles, is best able to calm and care for the herd. But wielding the flaming sword demands that we do our work, now and forever.

FINDING YOUR WAY

"I came to explore the wreck," wrote poet Adrienne Rich in *Diving into the Wreck*, "not the story of the wreck / the thing itself and not the myth."

We dive into the wreck, make our way to the back of the cave, to retrieve the treasure. We use our words, as Rich says, as maps to our purpose. Our radically inquisitive questions are spades. A leader's work, now and forever, is to turn the muck of the ocean bottom and find the way.

Dr. Sayres's questions gave me courage while honoring my cowardice, mapping my purpose and my way. Here are your spades, questions to ask yourself so that you might reboot your leadership and move forward on your journey of growing up.

- How would I act were I to remember who I am?

- What choices would I make, what actions would I take, if I regularly said the things that needed to be said?

- Who would I become were I to be fully, completely, and wholly heard?

- What is it that I wish the people in my life understood about me?

- Who would I be without the myths I've told about myself; the stories that took hold when I was yearning to feel love, safety, and belonging?

First, having turned that muck, we then create the embodiment of our wishes and dreams: our organizations, our communities, our society. So often I'm called in to help lead conversations about mission, value, and purpose. When, really, the only questions that matter are those that tell us who we are and wish to be.

- How would our organization respond were we to hear all the things that are being said, regardless if they are being said with words or deeds?

- What does it mean to be a leader at our organization?

- What does it mean to be grown, a fully actualized adult?

- How would we feel if our children were to work for the company we've created or the team we lead?

- How has the unsorted baggage of what has happened to us shaped who we are as leaders?

- When our employees and colleagues leave our sides and our company, what do we want them to say about our time together?

- What do we believe to be true about the world?

- What do we, as a community of people working toward a common goal, believe the world needs?

Regardless of the myths we are telling ourselves, what kind of company or organization are we truly building?

At the end of our days, are we becoming the person we'd like to be? A great, guiding point to that question is yet another question: What kind of adults do I want my children to be or become? Whoever that might be, we must be that person now, to map out the path of becoming that will help them, in their time, to do their work and retrieve their sunken treasure.

Parker and I had one of our epic conversations in which we laughed as much as we spoke. We came to realize that the only answer to the existential question of "Does my life have meaning?" is, again, another set of questions: "In what ways have I been brave?" And "How have I been kind?"

Only by standing still, asking ourselves such questions, and listening to the answers, will we finally find the warrior-leader within. Only then do we get to grow up and become the adults that are our birthright and responsibility. If we stand still, we may not like what we hear. We may be frightened by what our soul tells us: I don't want to be CEO. I don't want this life. I'm meant for something or someone else. Asking ourselves such open, honest questions takes courage, for the answers may frighten us, challenging our working belief systems. If we hear answers that surprise, confuse, and upset us, we'll have to confront a terrifying follow-on question: *"Now* what do I do?"

My friend Al Doan, the co-founder of the Missouri Star Quilt Company, stood still, turned over the muck, and decided to leave his job as CEO. A few months later he met Drea. They were married a year later.

Months after our rooftop beer toast, Chad and I sat still and silent. The pause in our conversation was lovely, deep, nourishing. Side by side, we watched his young son push a toy bulldozer through a sand pile at a Brooklyn playground and turned the soil of his transition out of Etsy. We laughed at his decreased need to vomit as a result of the stomach-churning roller-coaster ride of being a CEO. We laughed at the imagined fears of post-CEO life. We relished his relaxed ways and his ability to appreciate the slant of light, the smell of the rain, and the joy in hearing his son's delighted squeal—"Look, Dad, look!"—at some suddenly revealed magic. He then turned quiet and thoughtful as his son buried my hand in the sand of an imagined construction site. Chad turned to me with a realization of the true nature of post-CEO life: "Ya know," he said with a chuckle and a shake of his head, "once you're a leader, you're always a leader. You kinda have no choice. You can't put it back in the box."

"And I guess, once you're a warrior," I laugh in response,

"you're always a warrior. You don't really have a choice about that, either."

As I write these words, Chad has sent me text messages. He and his family are headed out for a long-wished-for cross-country drive. "All my new life infrastructure is working well," he wrote. "Sleeping well, have a great doctor, finances are humming, etc. Feeling good. Xoxo."

"This is how life is supposed to be," I wrote back. "This is what your son needs from his dad. Enjoy it." Even if you don't always act like it, I realize, once you're an adult, you're always an adult.

As I close out this chapter, I swap stories and old-man remembrances with my friend Steve Kane. I ask him, "Did you ever regret not taking Gamesville public?"

Not really, he tells me. "All my co-founders and I ever aspired to was to create a great business where we could have stimulating, enjoyable work for ourselves and our staff and make a great living." Good work, done well, for the right reasons.

"We were 'entrepreneurs' when all that meant was being lonely and scared and very different from everybody else we knew," he continues. Those folks "were busy working their way to success and prosperity, climbing up various ladders, not risking it all on some ambitious but super-risky idea." He adds, "We just wanted to be our own bosses and make a great living."

Most of us will spend our days in some sort of work. All of us lucky enough to be healthy will grow older. Those two realities give us a tremendous opportunity: use the work we need to perform to keep ourselves safe to grow into the adults we were born to be. The greatest gifts of leadership are its challenge to remember who we are and the opportunity to become the grown-ups we were meant to be.

AN ARTIST OF MY DAYS

For me, this has meant integrating words into my daily life. For the man I am meant to be is someone who understands the liberating power of words; others' as well as mine. This awareness began as so much of my growth began: during long stretches of alone time. In this case, it was while I would take the subway from my home in Queens to my high school in Brooklyn. I started high school while we still lived in Brooklyn. Then, in the middle of ninth grade, my freshman year and following a fight between my parents, my mother and I moved to Queens while my father and two of my brothers stayed back in Brooklyn. Technically, I violated the rules, as my high school was zoned only for those kids who lived in Brooklyn.

But with all the disruption in my life caused by my parents' separation, I didn't want to change schools as well. What's more, we were never sure how long this separation was going to last. Like many other aspects of our family life, it wasn't really discussed. One day, a few months later, my father and my brothers simply moved in with us.

That move changed my life. I began spending three hours a day commuting, most often alone. To pass the time, I would do my homework and I'd read. I first began reading *The Lord of*

the Rings on the A train from Lefferts Boulevard to Jay Street
in downtown Brooklyn. I escaped the pressures of the subway,
home, and the stress of the commute, and found a haven in
Middle-earth.

I found comfort in other worlds. By reading closely, I discovered that all writers—whether they were writing about
Frodo taking his seat as a broken-open-hearted warrior at the
gates of Mordor; or how Zorba (the Greek) melted into the grief
of his young son's death by dancing until his heart could cry no
more; or how the mysterious, unnamed Invisible Man savored
the sweetness of a hot-buttered yam on the streets of Harlem;
or how a "nicens little boy named baby tuckoo" would grow
into a young man and artist named Stephen Daedalus—were
essentially telling the same story: their own. While reading
others' words, I began to discover my own.

I remember once holding on to the train car pole as the A
train swayed sickeningly, reading of the twisted interplay between Raskolnikov and Svidrigailov in *Crime and Punishment*.
I was nauseated by Raskolnikov's struggles with his overwhelming guilt and his burning hatred for his foil, his coun-
terpart. I was so overcome with nausea that I had to grab the
first seat available. I put the book away and took out a black-
and-white "marble" composition book and began writing.
That was the beginning of a lifetime of journaling. That was
the beginning of finding my words.

This dance between the words of others and words of my
own deepened over the next few years. Early on in my commuting years, I learned to hack my journey. I shaved twenty
minutes off the long commute by exiting the subway, the

A train, at Jay Street, going above ground and walking a few blocks to the Lawrence Street station to get to the M train. I used my subway pass—something that enabled all students to ride the subways for free—to switch to the M train . . . the M bound for Coney Island . . . which would take me to the station closest to my high school.

Technically, this was a violation, as the pass was to be used only at my school and home stations, but that would have required riding the A into Manhattan, where I could switch to the M while remaining underground. My little hack created the conditions for yet another asteroid to hit me.

Each day, as I made my way from Jay to Lawrence, I'd pass Binkin's Books. One day I couldn't contain myself and I wandered in. Mr. Binkin sat wheezing behind a cash register and a pile of books. And there were books everywhere. Piles and piles of books. Dirty, dusty, musty books. I was in heaven; I'd found another haven. I'd visit Binkin's every day. I'd wander the aisles. Every now and then, someone would come in and ask Mr. Binkin if he had a certain book. "I have no idea!" he'd growl between wheezes. "Go find it yourself." Most folks would storm out.

One day I sat in the corner, my backpack at my feet. I had a boxed edition of *Ivanhoe* on my lap and was scribbling in my composition book, my journal. Suddenly Mr. Binkin came from behind his counter, shuffling and wheezing as he squeezed his considerable bulk past the musty piles. He tossed a book into my lap. "Here . . . you'll like this."

We had never spoken more than a word or two—usually just him telling me how much he was charging me for some tattered book I held at the counter. I think the most frequent thing I heard him say was, "Fifty cent." I looked down at my lap, and there was a tattered copy of *Call It Sleep* by Henry Roth.

Even then I knew that no matter how much I identified with him, I wasn't David Schearl, the main protagonist. The facts of our lives were just too different. But the feelings of our lives mirrored each other's. Later, when I was a man, I came to understand Roth's story and the poignant, painful story of his novel having been forgotten for decades, only to have been discovered in a remainder rack by a literary critic. Long after Roth had traded the life of an author for the life of a Maine woodsman and duck farmer, he remembered who he was, rediscovered his words, and overcame his wordlessness.

The twin asteroids of Binkin's and *Call It Sleep* helped me begin to find my words. For in my youngest days, I felt wordless, and that wordlessness led me to try to end my life. In retrospect, that attempt—at eighteen—wasn't merely a crying-out as folks are wont to say but a desperate attempt to speak, to cut through, to say what it was that needed saying.

Perhaps the trajectory of my leadership journey has been simply about learning to find the words. When I was a reporter, I looked to say what needed to be said about the world as I was experiencing it. Later, as an investor, it was my ability to clearly see the world that was emerging as well as the warriors within the entrepreneurs seeking funding that led me to whatever financial success and approbation I enjoyed.

Writing, coaching, teaching, being present, serving others—this is what I was meant to do. I am becoming the man I was meant to be. When I fail to live into that truth (as I assuredly and frequently do), I'm heeding the worn-out admonitions of my Loyal Soldiers and living from my shadow. Part of my trajectory has been learning to accept my frailties, shortcomings, and the myriad clever, insidious ways I act out the parts of me I'd rather not see. "Writing," notes the poet Terry Tempest Williams, "requires an aching curiosity leading you to discover, uncover, what is gnawing at your bones."

Retrieving those parts of me, uncovering what's been gnawing at my bones, has allowed me to find a source of strength, wisdom, and creativity. As I become more cognizant of the parts of me about which I can feel shame, I am more willing to admit to myself that I fail time and again to live up to the best aspirations, and as a result, my sense of spirit and worthiness grows. My great guide, the beloved poet John O'Donohue, reminds us, "Each of us is an artist of our days. The greater our integrity and awareness, the more original and creative our time will become."

Whatever the originality and creativity, whatever the leadership and adult wisdom that I carry, stem from the lessons I've learned from those who have come before me. For when I'm reading, I'm uncovering the truths they discovered. When I'm journaling, I'm discovering my own truth. When I'm writing, I'm speaking the truths that come from the synthesis of the truth of others and my own words, my own truth. To be a good leader, I've had to learn to be as honest as I could, facing down the shame-producing caws of the Crow. To be a good leader and a good writer has meant learning to be an honest, non-deluded adult. To be a good writer, I must be an honest man.

BUILDING CASTLES, SLAYING DRAGONS, AND REBOOTING ME

I can't think of a sadder way to die than with the knowledge that I never showed up in this world as who I really am. I can't think of a more graced way to die than with the knowledge that I showed up here as my true self, the best I knew how, able to engage life freely and lovingly because I had become fierce with reality.

—PARKER PALMER, *ON THE BRINK OF EVERYTHING*

"Why are you so obsessed with this good man thing?" Ali asked, her voice tinged with a mix of fear and frustration. She was tired of my groundlessness. Perhaps she saw in me what I often fail to see and so is upset by the stories I tell about myself and the questions that plague me.

What is a good man? Have I been a good father? Do I even have a superpower? Am I the impostor the Crow tells me I am? I turn over these questions repeatedly.

A good man takes care, answers a voice in my head; that of my father, perhaps, or my Grandpa Guido? A good man, as I've been repeating lately, builds castles, slays dragons, and, if he's opened his heart, tends the hearth—building a fire against the cold, empty night so that his loved ones are safe, warm, and happy. Hand-built castles and slain dragons give those he loves safety and belonging.

On a walk on a hill in Marin, thankful for the gift that is California, I met an ancient tree, toppled by age, blight, and wind. Stopping in my tracks, I realized, Here lies a good man.

If, at the end of my days, as this current meat bag starts its inevitable transition to the Earth that birthed me, I can lie as majestically about the soil as this elder, I'll know that I earned my manhood.

His body ragged with the scars of actions he may not always have been proud of but resting in the knowledge that for fifty, sixty, or one hundred years he grew into his purpose: sheltering others, providing them a respite from the glaring sun, the toppling wind, and the painful vagaries of life. Gnarled and twisted by inaction, decisions taken and not taken; scarred by selfishness, with limbs stretched by acts of kindness, generosity, and gentleness; I wish to end my days stretched out on the side of a hill, welcoming the slow decomposition of my anxieties and my flesh into nourishing earth.

Years ago, I had an epic dream—the kind that teaches you about yourself. I had returned to a past job, the place where I became an adult and a father. Working this gift from my innermost being, I found myself articulating fiercely my purpose: to serve others in their pursuit of their own becoming.

To do that, I've modeled myself after my teachers, stepping into their giant, impactful footsteps; they who taught me that the way to guide is to ask and not to tell. There's an indescribable power in a well-asked question; questions that are open-ended and honest (honest in that I couldn't know the answer) allow my clients' souls to speak.

When they ask me how to be a better leader, I'll often ask them to tell me what they think it means to lead well. "How should I build my company?" is met with "What kind of company do you want to work for?"

I know I frustrate them. Like my being frustrated by Ani

Pema Chödrön's advice to follow the "pathless path," I know they simply want answers. And beyond sharing my observations about my own journey, and my own lessons learned, all I can offer is questions.

What kind of leader are you? Tell us and teachers will guide you, reflecting when you're leading with congruency. For me, I'm a leader who relies on the power of words to convey meaning and purpose, to find the empathy that allows a team to coalesce and cohere.

Tell me what success and failure mean for you and we can use your answers to chart a path. Tell me if, after imagining your children working for your company, you feel shame, fear, or pride, and I'll tell you if you're building a worthwhile company.

What do you believe about the world? Is the world a harsh, dog-eat-dog world or is it, despite its obvious failings, a life-giving generative gift from the divine? What do you believe about people? Are they out to optimize only for themselves or are they simply stalled, blocked by the ghosts in their machines, waiting to be led to a place of full actualization, full growth, into warrior adulthood?

Back on that hill in Marin, the toppled tree brings me back to the chestnut tree of my childhood—my friend, my sanctuary. I weep at the comparison. This gnarled oak got to live out its days while my friend ended in a pile of sawn logs and dust. At its base, near where the massive root system had been ripped from the earth, irises were sprouting. I want then to be reborn with the bright promise of young irises. A good man, a good leader, a warrior, a grown-up takes pride in his aspirations without using failure to achieve those aspirations as evidence of his unworthiness, his unlovability. He also gives that to his children, his loved ones, his partners, his friends, his colleagues, and all those whom he encounters.

I think again of my proofreader dad's Parker pen, the one he'd use to complete the puzzles in the *Daily News*, the one he'd use to correct the typos in the paper, the one that never left his side. I loved that pen, for I saw in it an instrument of his care and his efforts to be a good man. Abandoned as a baby and given over for adoption, he, like my mother, did the best he could. I think of Mom's weekly deposits to her Christmas club savings account—a dollar here, five dollars there—saving and saving so that, come Christmas, she could buy us the toys that would make us squeal with delight. One of the sweetest, most joyful memories of my life is of my brothers Dom, John, and me tearing the wrapping off our matching aluminum suitcase-style play sets: Dom got the Viking set, John the frontier fort, and I got the miniature space-travel launch center with "real" rockets that sent astronauts to the moon and exploring asteroids and shooting stars.

Mom and Dad were, of course, both toppled by age and illness; their bodies, hearts, and minds bore the scars and twisted limbs of the vagaries of life. Those two may have been gnarled and twisted by their fears and the violence of the abandonment and anger of those who came before them, but their limbs were also stretched by acts of kindness, generosity, and the tremendous courage and will to do right by their children and grandchildren.

A few weeks before my son Michael was to turn twenty-one,

he and I sat down at a table. He stared off into the backyard of what was the home in which he and his brother, Sam, and sister, Emma, had come of age. Staring off, we spoke of the fearful potential of his life. The awful and awe-filled possibilities as he imagined his future life, with his college years ending and the rest of his years beginning. He laughed when I shared the title of Parker's latest book, *On the Brink of Everything.* "That's it!" he said. "That's exactly how I feel." Parker, writing about life from the vantage point of his late seventies, had spoken to a young man, a good man, in his early twenties. On the brink of everything and facing the future, with fear, tenacity, excitement, and curiosity.

This is how we grow. Irises sprouting at the base of the toppled-over sage tree, one who's served the world well and is taking his deserved rest dying in such a graced way.

BECOMING ME

My pursuit of lemon drops and Monopoly money had left me wealthy but empty. When I was circling the street above the stinking, smoking hole of Ground Zero, I hadn't yet put to rest the ghosts in the machine of my childhood. Money in my pocket did little to quiet the lingering shame and guilt I felt, watching my father blow air into an empty wallet when I asked for the funds to apply to college.

No matter the success I had, no matter the headlines I garnered, I couldn't quiet the warnings of my Loyal Soldier, who whispered the misplaced, childlike logic that, to save myself, I had to deplete myself; that to belong, to be safe, to be loved, I had to die. I was trapped by this logic. It seemed that the only way to earn what I had, the only way to earn *it*—the approbations, the lemon drops, the safety I sought, the right to see myself as an adult, a good man—was to give and give like the fairytale gingerbread man being eaten by the fox: "I'm a quarter gone . . . I'm half gone . . . I'm three-quarters gone . . . I'm all gone!"

But the rebooting of my internal systems helped me understand that the world isn't a fox out to eat us. The world doesn't really want to harm us at all. It may wish to shape us, to change us into something other than who we were born to be. It will give us facile playbooks on how to be a leader. It'll give us subtle and gross signs that we are not what it needs us to be. But it isn't out to eat us. It merely wants from us the ability to fill the hole in its chest.

Like each of us, our colleagues, our lovers, our friends all want love, safety, and belonging. They merely, unconsciously, see in us the potential to meet that need. So, we become the objects of their projections, the screen onto which they project their own shadows. Wanting to belong, we cooperate. We become our employees' disapproving parent, the foil in their comedy act, the fun-house mirror reflecting the view of them they want to see, the partner against whom they struggle so that they can grow. We become their Irrational Other, so they can stumble, skin their knees, and find their own way. In this way, the world can ask us to give more and more until there's less and less of us. Perversely, then we are often rewarded for our complicity in this dance. Lemon drops and the envy of others can be ours for the taking.

The world affirmed me for giving more and more, for

allowing my hair to catch and remain on fire, for giving and giving until I became the gingerbread man. I gave because I wanted to belong. But the more I gave, the more I lost. And the more lost I became.

Yet we are more than the ghosts in our machines. We can stand still, power down, reboot the systems, and disrupt the programing. We need to have the courage to be truthful and break through our delusions and accept the "this being so" of life.

I will always be haunted by lemon drops, sawdust, and the power of words. I am grateful this is so. Out of such pain, such suffering, and the muck and mud of my ocean bottom, a tall, strong tree of a man has emerged. I overcame the wordlessness of my youth. I became a good man by learning to love words—first, those of others; then, later, my own words. I became who I was born to be by learning to read and then, later, to write. I learned that a life well written is a life well led. I became a good leader and I'm still becoming a good man. That is my legacy: the wisdom of knowing that the act of becoming a good man is more important than arriving at that place. With that, I've begun mastering the art of growing up.

Journaling Invitations

How will I know my work is done?

———

Afterword:
A Light Heart Lives Long

As this book came alive, life's roller coaster continued unabated. In the just more than a year since I began writing, one friend married the love of his life while two others divorced. The parents, grandparents, children, and spouses of various friends all struggled with illness and death.

For example, as I was finding my way to my words, my brother Vito was temporarily silenced with painful throat cancer. When we were very young, Vito had introduced me and my brothers, John and Dom, to Winnie-the-Pooh. Dom, John, and I would climb over and around my big brother's lap, laughing as Vito read of Pooh knowing no other way to come down the stairs than upside down and with his head banging on each step ("silly old bear"). We laughed with the love, safety, and belonging of our snuggling in our big brother's lap.

Now, decades later, as I write these words on a crisp September morning, Vito has rediscovered his words; he e-mails the family, "The doctor says I'm cancer free."

In March 2018, I flew to California. My plane landed, and my phone buzzed with news I'd been dreading for close to a year: Dr. Sayres had died. As the plane made its way over the tarmac to the gate, as the other passengers gathered their belongings, I sat still. I wept. Grief washed over me; she who is so present in this work, I thought, will never know the completed book.

Around the same time, I was seated at a conference table at my doctor's office when the young internist came in to review the scan of my heart. "If it were me," he said with his Adam's apple bobbing, "I'd get a stent, preferably as soon as possible." With that shock coursing through my body, I boarded a plane to spend the weekend in Providence, visiting my son Michael at school. The doctor's words haunted me the whole of the flight: "If it were me, I'd get a stent."

The next day, Michael and I strolled Thayer Street, stopping at the Brown University bookstore. I was still clouded with shock, grief, and fear. At the checkout counter, as I paid for a copy of Marie Ponsot's latest collection of poetry and, for Michael, a copy of *A Portrait of the Artist as a Young Man*, I caught sight of a tiny button with black lettering on a white field: A LIGHT HEART LIVES LONG . . . I stood next to one of my children—source of the fierce calling to be my most adult self—and wept once more. This time, though, I wept at the wonderful synchronicity of life.

In the months since I opened myself to writing this book, an excavation of the relationship between leadership and the act of becoming an adult, my heart has been broken several times. With a cardiologist's blessing, I chose not to get the stent. My writing became my stent, keeping the arteries of my broken heart open. My words, like my blood, flowed freely. A light heart that lives long is one that has learned to appreciate the roller coaster from the ground, to see that the point of it all is to know that life simply goes on. And, as my father once joked, the alternative to life not going on "isn't that great."

The synchronicity wasn't manifested in my finding a button with a message I needed to hear at precisely the moment I needed to hear it. The synchronicity lay in the testing of my core thesis precisely as I was writing that thesis.

It was as if life itself were asking me if I truly believed my own simple assertion about life and leadership. What better way for the universe to test my belief—that better humans make better leaders—than to send me on a roller-coaster ride of heartbreak, challenging me to be a better human? For the patterns we developed to keep ourselves from feeling suffering and the pain of broken hearts are what hold each of us back from being our most adult selves, the best leaders possible.

I had to stand still and show up fully and keep showing up despite my butt being kicked and my heart being broken.

"[T]o speak of such things without being willing to reveal your own actualization, your own journey to adulthood would be hollow and empty," I wrote in the introduction, "Hollow and empty would not suffice." That remained true, even as my butt was kicked and my heart ached.

Sharon Salzberg, my mogul of lovingkindness, bore witness

to the butt kicking. As the great teacher that she is, Sharon helped me see that all things were workable. Every bit of the experience—every joy and every vomit-inducing drop on the roller coaster—is an opportunity to practice and to grow. I honor her teachings when I remember that the art of growing up includes the practice of remembering that all beings are basically good. Such remembering, the late poet John O'Donohue reminds us, is an essential element of adult leadership. "When someone fails or disappoints you," he writes, "May the graciousness with which you engage / Be their stairway to renewal and refinement."

All things are workable. Every dip and rise of the roller coaster, every instance of heartbreak and life unfolding, are opportunities for that radical inquiry within. In this way, we turn the experience of being a leader into the journey into adulthood. In this way, says O'Donohue, leadership becomes, "a true adventure of growth."

The goal of this book was to act on you as a coaching session might. The goal was to give you something more useful than answers: the ability to work with the questions, the uncertainties, and the doubts that spring from the dips in life. To show you that you could arrive at your own answers; answers that would be authentic and true to you. At some point you may find doubts arising. At some point, if you're at all like the rest of us, you may ask yourself if you're even able to participate in that true adventure of growth. If so, know that the answer is a resounding yes. But there's a catch. It's yes, but only if you're willing to put your head up to the mouth of the demon. In this case, the demon is the underlying lack of belief in your capacity to lead. The demon's teeth are powerful questions, the answers to which frighten and startle you, accelerating your growth.

This path to adult leadership demands that such fearful questions are answered fearlessly. To do this, we notice our responses, with discerning inquiry and without judgment, to the questions that arise. Inquiring this way isn't, as some may fear, a form of indulgent navel gazing but a fearsome first step in the resolution to grow. Indeed, therein lies another opportunity for leadership growth: What might my reluctance about looking inward say about the protective patterns of my life? How might such a reticence be shaping my organization and our ability to consider alternative possibilities? What do the ghosts in my machine tell me about the risks posed by opening myself or standing firm while others open themselves? What do those ghosts need to hear to finally rest in peace?

There's a tradition in Buddhism of dedicating the merit of any effort we undertake. In this way, we believe, all actions may be of service to others. In honor of that tradition, may whatever merit my effort has generated be of service to you. Moreover, may the merit generated by your seeking answers to powerful, open, and honest questions about your life and your leadership be of service to those you lead. In the end, if I've managed to convince you that better humans make better leaders, then your open, honest questions are simple: "What is my work to do to become a better human?" "What kind of leader am I?" And, finally, "What kind of adult am I meant to be?"

AUTHOR'S NOTE

Here's to the imperfection of memory. Here's to the way we "fiction and fable our lives," as the poet Pádraig Ó Tuama, says, "in order to tell of things that are more than true." To complete this work, to show up in a way that is not hollow and empty, I had to tap the wellspring of my imperfect and fabling memory.

How many stitches did I get at the top of my head after I slipped walking down the steps into our house while wearing my roller skates? Was it six or sixteen times that the needle went into my skin at the top of my skull? Was the bike I received at eight in celebration of my First Holy Communion red or purple?

The imperfection of remembering past things is often coupled with the need to fiction and fable. I tried to meet this need and to do well by mixing composite and real, named characters. For to live well, notes my friend Pádraig, "is to see wisely and to see wisely is to tell stories."

Indeed, some folks' stories have been disguised while others have been left out. In fact, there were far more folks absented than included. The many partners, co-founders, significant others, and family members have been left out not out of malice but simply by my best judgment. The times and places of events have been altered in ways to support the underlying message, to support the demand to say the more-than-true things.

The result is a collection of stories made visceral by my imperfect memories and observations. I am, after all, Holder of Stories of the Heart, and we are a tribe of warriors sitting around a campfire, using tales to make sense of an insensible world.

There are those folks whose lives I touch upon who surely have different feelings, observations, and perceptions. Such different views are no less true or valid than my own. While the facts remembered by others may be different, our feelings are doubtlessly similar; maybe even more than true. The wise elders in my life encouraged me to honor such different feelings, such different truths, as I honor my own.

I've tried to use my truth to advance an understanding of the world as I've come to see it. What's required of each of us, I believe, is to speak truth while releasing ourselves from the obligation to share the *whole* truth.

This said, and for what it's worth, the bike was purple, and it had a great banana seat.

ACKNOWLEDGMENTS

Many authors acknowledge the people in their lives who helped make their book a reality. When I read that a book would not have been possible were it not for the acknowledged folks, I'd always assumed such statements were merely polite hyperbole. Then I wrote my own book. Now I know what those writers felt.

For example, this book benefitted from the support and patience of Ali Schultz.

Ali, you supported me through each word of every draft. You patiently listened to me read aloud passage after passage, encouraging me as I'd edit on the fly. Far too many Sunday-evening dinners were spent with my frustrated declarations of utter incompetence after a weekend of vain attempts to write. You stared me down and brooked no nonsense when I'd lament that I was never going to finish, that I was a fool for even trying, and that I should just send back the advance. You pushed me forward when my Crow squawked his loudest. Indeed, you've always seen the good in me, especially when my fears caused me to see only my failings.

Even today you continue to tether me, keeping me grounded to the reality of who I am and the good work I do, and when I am lost and wishing for nothing more than to disappear into the crack of the tree, you show me the way home. Thank you for being my map and my anchor.

Dear Sam, Emma, and Michael: Of all the things I've done in my life, nothing compares to the experience of being your father. It is a gift that grows in depth and meaning every day. I am breathless and in awe of the wonderful adults you've become, and will be forever grateful for the honor of being your parent.

To my brothers and sisters, thank you for allowing me to share my version of our story. It is, of course, my version. But knowing that I had your love and support made diving into the wreck of our shared past easier:

- Vito, thank you not only for Christopher Robin and Edward Bear, but for teaching all of us that words and music together can move us to be more than shattered souls. Thanks, too, for trying to teach Dad to love jazz as much as you do. ("I don't get this music," he said. "It has no beginning, no middle, no end." "Exactly," said Vito, smiling.)

- Mary, way too early in a young girl's life, you stepped into the role of caring for all of us, your siblings. Thank you. You listened to each of us and encouraged us to find our own voices. You gave me *Madeline* and *The Story of Babar: The Little Elephant* and opened me to the world of poetry. You saw in a scared, often wordless little boy his desire and love for words.

- Nicki, my fierce, loving sister. Your steadfast resolve and unflinching regard for doing right by the world gifted me with a deep appreciation for justice in the world. In doing so, you kept me safe, helped me feel loved, and showed me time and again that I belonged.

- Annie, who early on told me to "write every day," thank you for opening me up to Ani Pema Chödrön and Parker Palmer. You gave me the gift of their words at precisely the moment when my heart was broken open enough to allow those words to fall in. Thanks, too, for reading the very first short story I ever wrote, *Chrysalis Broken*, and for encouraging me to keep finding my words.

- Dom, you never, ever stopped questioning the world and wondering why it can't be more than what it is. In doing so, you taught me the power of wisdom and inquiry. More than that, though, you gave me late nights eating fresh-popped popcorn, watching old movies on a black-and-white TV, and staying up late to watch Yankee games. Thank you for teaching me that it's far wiser to be a Yankee fan than a Mets fan.

- John . . . so many of my best memories include you: repairing school lockers on hot summer days and extracting a broken drill bit from my thumb; visiting the Brooklyn Museum to try to sketch mosaic Roman ducks for our art class at Queens College; and building the darkroom out of Grandpa Colonna's wine cellar. Thank you for always, always having my back.

To my grandparents and great-grandparents: *Sangue del mio sangue. Gra*z*ie per i vostri sacrifici. Onoro tutto ciò che avete rinunciato per poter parlare al posto vostro.* And, to my father's birth mother: *Go raibh maith agat as saol m'athar.*

Dear Sharon Salzberg, thank you for the kind words that open this work. More, though, thank you for being my friend and my teacher. I will do my best to honor your care by striving to help others every day and to live out the meaning of lovingkindness.

To my fellow Reboot-ers: It's difficult to describe the joy that comes from knowing that we've built a company that lives up to that which we teach our clients. To Khalid Halim and Dan Putt, thank you for trusting me when I said, "Hey, guys . . . I have an idea. . . ." To Andy Crissinger, Zane Altman, Chris VandenBrink, Courtney Joyce, and Albert Lee, thank you for joining this band of warriors in the revolution to bring love, soul, and magic into companies. To Margaret Hendricks, who embodies the notion of superpowers.

To Jim Marsden, my once and future Pathfinder, thank you

for your kindness, wisdom, and grace; Big Love to you, forever.

I can't mention Reboot without adding my deep and abid-
ing thanks to all the coaches with whom we have the great
honor to work. Our work is sacred; thank you for your efforts
to help leaders grow.

Over the decades, I have had good friends who have taught
me about the world. From my childhood, there are Phil Levy,
Danny Zogott, and Jeff Oppenheim, with whom I began to
explore the world beyond my family. Years later we discovered
just how much we had in common. Later in my life came Jeff
Walker, Tracey Durning, Jenn McCrea, Carrie and Kirsten
Barry, Ann Mehl (who first challenged me to come out of my
post–investor years exile), and Seth Godin, who's taught me
so much over the decades of our friendship, not the least of
which is the liberation of a page left intentionally blank.

There's also Tamdin Wangdu, who took me to Tibet, to
touch the ground from which my soul was birthed. Linnea
Passaler and Alessio Santo, who took me to Palo del Colle to
feel the ground that birthed my grandparents. There's Mark
Pincus, who brought me to Fred Wilson, convincing me to
consider being his partner. There's Kerri Rachlin; Kerri, for
nearly twenty years you've been my soul sister. Thank you for
looking out for me, especially when my depression would get
the best of me (as it so often did). There's Ben Saunders, who,
time and again, helps me understand the depths of bravery and
the possibilities in dreaming.

And of course, there are Fred Wilson and Brad Feld.

Fred taught me more than the business of venture capital;

he taught me about steadfastness, discernment, and leading with values, especially when the judgment call was painful. Brad, my brother, you taught me the value of a good walk and showed me the value of wisdom by having the incredible good sense to have married Amy Batchelor. We need to sit again on your porch, my friend, and watch the sun set.

This book would not have come into being had it not been for the love and trust of the hundreds of people who asked me to hold their stories, as clients, as guests on my podcast, or as attendees at a workshop or boot camp. These include: Tracy Lawrence, Al Doan, Kent Cavendar-Barres, Jeff Orlowski, Bryce Roberts, Bijan Sabet, Yancey Strickler, Amy Nelson, Virginia Bauman, Khe Hy, Natalie McGrath, Patty McCord, Semil Shah, Tarikh Korula, Bobby Brannigan, Matt Tara, Ben Rubin, Dan Harris, Nancy Lublin, Adi Mashiach, Sally Spencer-Thomas, Adeesh Agarwal, Derek Flanzraich, Erin Frey and Ti Zhao, Ian Hogarth, Jud Brewer, Nicole Glaros, Melissa Pasquale, Shelly Francis, Reverend Michelle Haunold Lorenz, Leonie Akhidenor, Simon Cant, Matt Munson, Cat Hoke, James Hollis, Alex Blumberg, Matt Lieber, Isaac Oates, Sarah Weiler, Amir Salihefendic, Konda Mason, Nicholas Russell, John Guydon, Dave Zwieback, Mary Lemmer, Representative Tim Ryan, Patrick Campbell, Richard Hughes-Jones, Henry May, Chris Marks, Evgeny Shadchnev, Zoe Weintraub, Joanne Domeniconi and Jules Pieri, Hugh MacLeod, Sherman Lee, Bill Morrison, Tanisha Robinson, Nigel Sharp, Dave Otten, Jeroen Wijering, Brian Rivkin, Vince Horn, Derek Bereit, Beth McKeon, Blaine Vess, Rand Fishkin, Carm Huntress, Joe Chura, Joe Bassett, and Duncan Morris.

My gratitude to each of you; you honored me by asking me to hold your hearts for a bit.

Others who have helped along the way include Adam Grant, David Cohen, Jason Calacanis (who, many years ago, helped Fred Wilson and me be a little smarter about investing), Jeff Lawson, Jessi Hemphill (who told a few folks the story of the man who makes founders cry), Kurt Andersen, Matt Stinchomb, Scott Kriens, and Tim Ferris. Thank you all.

For more years then I can recall, Wednesday mornings have been special, for I joined a group of people to laugh, cry, and radically inquire within. Together we've lived up to the assignment that Dr. Sayres gave us: to be adults. Thank you, Steve Padnick, Rory Rothman, Linda Peltz, Joan Hertz, and Phoebe Snochat for bearing witness to my finally growing up. I love each of you.

Whatever wisdom I may share is merely a transmission of the teachings I've received. I've spoken before of Parker Palmer, but it's important to note here the profound importance of his work as a teacher. Parker, you continue to show so many the way to be adult in the world. Thank you.

In addition to Sharon Salzberg and Ani Pema, other teachers who have helped me include Roshi Joan Halifax and Jerry Ruhl. Jerry Ruhl, a good and kind man whose works taught me profound insights long before we met in real life. Jerry, your books, *Living Your Unlived Life* and *Contentment*, were turning points in my life. Thank you for writing them and thank you for being you.

I'm also deeply grateful for the works of David Whyte, Mary Oliver, James Hollis, David Richo, and John Welwood, all talented thinkers and writers. Writers and teachers such as these can be asteroids, forever changing the trajectories of our lives.

Other such asteroids include Jeff Levitsky, who, while I was still in high school, introduced me to Nikos Kazantzakis, Fyodor Dostoyevsky, and Ralph Ellison. "When I discover who I am," wrote Ellison, "I'll be free." Thank you, Mr. Levitsky, for helping me to discover who I am and, with that, become free.

I'm grateful to Professor Robert Greenberg for awarding me a scholarship that kept me going at Queens College, and to Lilo Leeds, as well as her husband, Gerry, for not only providing that scholarship but, later, embodying openhearted leadership. Lilo was the best boss I've ever had.

It should be recognized that creating a book is a collective act, and no writer could have had a better collaborator than Hollis Heimbouch. Hollis, you are a gift to writers everywhere. Jim Levine, my agent, was and remains a steadfast and kind soul, mirroring back exactly what my writer soul needed to hear to keep going. Thanks, too, to the whole team at HarperCollins. I appreciate all you do to preserve the craft of publishing and to bring forth books that change lives.

The collaboration, though, of course went beyond editors and writers. Krista Tippett, Brad Feld, Steve Kane, and Chad Dickerson each worked the lump of clay of the first drafts of the manuscript (the "shitty first draft" as Anne Lamott says) and helped me see what needed to be kneaded, what needed to be added, and—most important—what needed to be cut. Your suggestions made the shitty first draft better. Thank you.

Doubtless, there are dozens more people I should have

acknowledged. Any oversight stems purely from my own dis-tractedness and not from malice.

Finally, there were folks in my life who specifically asked not to be included in this work. Your wishes deserve to be honored. Nevertheless, I'll take a moment to honor all that you have meant not only to me but to those whom I love as well. I'll remain grateful to you forever.

Lastly, the next time I pick up a book, I'm going to start by reading the acknowledgments. That will be my small way of recognizing how difficult it is to write one.

Jerry Colonna is the CEO and co-founder of Reboot.io, an executive coaching and leadership development firm whose coaches and facilitators are committed to the notion that better humans make better leaders. For nearly twenty years, he has used the knowledge gained as an investor, executive, and board member at more than one hundred organizations to help entrepreneurs and others lead with humanity, resilience, and equanimity. Prior to his career as a coach, he was a partner with JPMorgan Partners (JPMP), the private-equity arm of JP Morgan Chase. He joined JPMP from Flatiron Partners, which he launched in 1996 with Fred Wilson. Flatiron became one of the most successful early-stage investment programs in the New York City area. He lives in Boulder, Colorado.